ON THE EAST END

THE LAST BEST TIMES OF A LONG ISLAND FISHING COMMUNITY

On The East End

The Last Best Times of a Long Island Fishing Community

Clarence R. Hickey

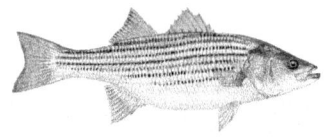

LongIslandNature.org

Harbor Electronic Publishing
| Sag Harbor, New York |
HEPDigital.com

2015

© 2015 Clarence R. Hickey

Library of Congress Control Number: 2015933103

ISBN 978-0-9740201-2-9 (paper)

ISBN 978-0-9740201-3-6 (eBook)

All rights reserved. No part of this publication may be reproduced, stored in a retrieval system, or transmitted in any form or by any means without the prior permission of Harbor Electronic Publishing. Permission is granted to photocopy any part of the book under contract with the Copyright Clearance Center (copyright.com).

Printed in the United States of America.

First printing: May 2015.

Cover photo by Kathryn Szoka
oneeyeopenkathrynszoka.wordpress.com

A Note on the Type: *On the East End* is set in Minion Pro, an Adobe Originals typeface designed by Robert Slimbach. It was inspired by classical, old-style typefaces of the late Renaissance, a period of elegant, beautiful, and highly readable type designs. The caption font is Gill Sans. Designed by Eric Gill, it is the Helvetica of England: ubiquitous and utilitarian.

For those fishermen and fishes
who fed me for a lifetime

Contents

Introduction	11
Another Year	21
A Nostalgic Trip Home	24
Something's Wrong with the Water	27
Of Baymen and Striped Bass	33
Striped Bass and Mae West	34
Listening	36
The Baymen's Association	41
Bass on the Backside	50
Resource Conflicts	54
Science and Society	57
Ocean Haul Seining	62
Respect and Generosity	67
The East End's Influence	69

Of Brookers and Bonackers	75
Rebuilding Fish Stocks and a Human Community	76

Fishing with Jimmy — 81

On Days of No Weather	84
There's Weather Today	87
Studying Montauk's Fish Diversity	92
Tending Jimmy's Traps	96
Fun, Educational, Never Dull	102

On the Sound — 113

Kyma	115
Lady Barbara	120
Leaky *Louise*	126
Catching and Sampling Live Animals	129
Live Animals and Ethical Challenges	133

The Last Best Times? — 143

Vigor of the Fishing Community	144
Vigor of the Local Scientific Community	151
"Man-to-Man" Must Come First	153
Community Among Resource Users	157
Compliance, Coercion, and Conservation	161
Like a Wild Mustang	166

Eagles and Aborigines — 169

Bibliography & End Notes — 175

Introduction

This is a book I have wanted to write for some time, and I began doing so more than 25 years ago. It started as an article for the *East Hampton Star* in 1985, *The Star*'s 100th year. The article, titled "Ocean Sciences Reminiscences" was a reflection and remembrance of the former New York Ocean Science Laboratory on Montauk where I worked as a young marine biologist from 1970–1975. The "Lab," as we employees called it, was a new institution in 1970, a consortium of eight colleges and universities that conducted oceanographic research and taught marine science.

The Lab was located on 36 acres of beach front property along the southern shore of Montauk's Fort Pond Bay, which fronts Block Island Sound on the eastern tip of Long Island's South Fork. The consortium was named Affiliated Colleges and Universities, Inc., with the member institutions being Adelphi, Fordham, Hofstra, Long Island, New York, and St. John's Universities, plus the New York Institute of Technology, and the State University of New York. It was full of promise and energy when it brought me to the East End right after I completed my master's degree in marine science at Long Island University. That was the fall of 1970. For the next four and half

On the East End

years my wife and I lived on the East End of Long Island and worked among the local people. She was a high school biology teacher in Sag Harbor, a graduate student at Long Island University, and an employee in the East Hampton Town Sea Food Producers Cooperative, Inc. in Amagansett. I was a marine biologist working, researching, and teaching at the Lab. Living in Amagansett and working at the Lab gave me the most wonderful opportunities to meet and know many of the traditional East End and Long Island fishermen and their families. They are the baymen and Bonackers who are the reason for this book.

My 1985 *East Hampton Star* article was based on a visit I made back to the Lab a couple of years after it had closed for good in 1982. We were living in Maryland then and were visiting friends in Amagansett. I drove onto Montauk to see the Lab's former director Dr. John Baiardi, with whom I had always enjoyed a nice relationship. He lived off Tuttle Road on the eastern cliffs of Fort Pond Bay. He and I went to the Lab site where its 36 acres and all of its buildings still were in tact. But there was no stir of human activity. Dr. Baiardi unlocked the old fisheries science buildings for me, where I worked and where I wrote several papers on East End fishes and fisheries. I walked through its corridors, now empty and quiet. As Henry David Thoreau did with the old and defunct neighborhood structures during his walks in the woods around Walden Pond in the 1840s, in my mind I, too, "repeopled" the landscape of that old lab building as I walked the emptiness of its corridors. It was an eerie feeling and quite sad. It was after the emptiness of that visit I wrote the *Star* article about the Lab, and I've always been struck that it was published on October 31, 1985—Halloween.

Toward the end of my tenure at the Lab in the mid-1970s, a new and modern fisheries laboratory building was being built. It never was fully completed before I departed the East End in September 1975. I envisioned in my mind a new office and lab space there, with a window looking out over Fort Pond Bay. In my mind's eye, I could

Introduction

look out that window, westerly, across the Bay and see bayman Jimmy Lester tending his pound traps. I fished with Jimmy many times during my Lab days, and for several years afterwards during visits back on the East End. Jimmy and I became good friends and we wrote several papers on the fishes he caught in his Fort Pond Bay trap nets. All of those papers are mentioned in this book and cited in the bibliography section at the end. I donated copies of all my scientific writings on Long Island and East End fishes to the public libraries in East Hampton, Amagansett, and Montauk. These papers may be found in the East Hampton Library Long Island Collection by searching online at www.easthamptonlibrary.org/history/index.html.

After my *East Hampton Star* article in 1985, I began writing what I hoped would be a book on my East End experiences, the baymen I knew, and the landscape and the estuarine waters of the East End. I wanted to capture the stories and adventures I had with fishermen and the fishing community. I wanted to make known the voices of people recently silenced, people who still speak to me through the lessons they taught and the lives they lived. The first chapter I penned off then was about fishing with Jimmy. While it appears here as chapter 3, it will always be first in my mind and heart. I continued to reflect on my East End time and picked away at two more chapters on my old electric typewriter. One chapter was on my experiences studying striped bass, working with the ocean haul seiners, and becoming a member of the East Hampton Town Baymen's Association.

The other was a recounting of having studied, researched, and worked on Long Island Sound. I had many memorable experiences and adventures on the Sound with fishes, fishermen, and aboard several research vessels and fishing boats. Long Island Sound, coupled with the East End, has influenced my professional work life and my very being ever since. Fishing and sampling on the Sound in some traditional western-rigged draggers taught me what it was like to work on the water, including the thrill of catching fish, and the chill and danger of nearly capsizing while dragging.

On the Sound, I tested some of my emerging and burgeoning concerns for the ethical treatment of fishes during field sampling. I had been fishing with bayman Jimmy Lester on Montauk for a few years and liked being able to release alive from his pound nets those fishes that were not going to market. So I translated some of that fishing behavior to my work on the Sound and I struggled a bit to make it work.

This little book, thus, in being my recollections of the East End and my experiences with the fishing community I knew there, is a bit autobiographical, sometimes a bit more than I like. But, it needs to be so, in order to capture and explain the fishing community, the East End, and its environment as I observed them while living among them in the early 1970s. I do this with original text and original photographs and figures. I have not sought great quality photos elsewhere to illustrate the subjects, but rather used those in my collection and in my possession because they are real to me and bring back the excitement and the emotion of the stories they tell and support. They show the East End as I saw it and knew it then.

It is fortunate that I wrote those three chapters, on the baymen, fishing with Jimmy, and Long Island Sound, twenty-plus years ago while the memories and feelings still were fresh and alive, and while I still was making annual visits to the East End to see old friends and reacquaint with the landscape and with the sea, which also were my good friends. If I had not done so, I doubt it could be done today, as the accounts of my working on the water and living on the East End probably could not be dragged up with as much good detail and spirit.

When I began writing this book in earnest in 2006, I took those three original typewritten chapters to a local printer in Rockville, Maryland, and had them scanned onto a computer disc in a format

Introduction

that enabled me to update, rewrite, and edit them in MS Word on my word processor. I then went back though my myriad of color slides and old photos from the 1970s. I have literally thousands of slides, most taken with my trusty old Kodak Instamatic pocket camera that went with me everywhere. Other photos in my collection were taken by my friend, fellow fisher, and Lab associate Carl Mamay. Carl was the Lab's staff photographer. I had the slides digitized and the photos scanned so that I could enhance and edit them on my PC. So, this book project became a collaboration of the scenes captured 30–35 years ago by camera, the memories and emotions captured twenty-five years ago by old typewriter and aging biologist, and the technology of today that enabled me to combine those with the observations and views that only time can render.

I am amazed and thankful for those old slides and photos, because they also enable me to tell these stories a bit differently and to an entirely new and different audience. I have converted many of those digitized slides into PowerPoint presentations and use them in the public schools in Maryland for talks on environmental science, environmental protection and stewardship, and marine biology careers. In the 1970s, when I was taking those slides with my pocket camera, never did I envision that 35 years hence I would still be using them, and to educate young people. Carl Mamay's photos made me look good during public and professional society presentations while I was on the East End in the 1970s, and they still are doing so today, even after the Lab's demise in 1982, and Carl's passing in 2000. Thanks, Bub.

When a decent draft of the manuscript was completed in 2007, I sought the advice and comment on it from two old friends on the East End, both of whom figure into the stories and adventures captured here. Byron Young is a fisheries and wildlife biologist extraordinaire with whom I associated for several years. Now retired from the New York State Department of Environmental Conservation, Byron lives yet on the East End and continues to be involved in local conservation and environmental matters, now volunteering his experience, time and talents. Edwin Sherrill is a baymen with much experience in both fishing and local government. I asked Byron and Ed to read my draft manuscript for factual accuracy and to offer comment about any matter therein. I did not ask either to agree with anything I wrote or with any of my observations, conclusions, or recommendations. I really wanted a sanity check on my recollections of the 1970s on the East End, especially regarding the commercial fishing community. Byron and Ed offered many comments and much constructive criticism, which I considered during the completion of the manuscript. They are friends, indeed, whom I much admire and whose council I very much appreciate. The ideas, observations, conclusions, and recommendations in this book, however, remain mine solely and I assume all responsibility for any mistakes that may have survived.

This book recounts the fishing community and many of the fishes I encountered on the East End as I observed them in the 1970s. I have not attempted to describe, or to annotate, in detail the history of the several centuries old fishing community there. That was done admirably and wonderfully by Peter Matthiessen in his 1986 book *Men's Lives: The Surfman and Baymen of the South Fork*. John Cole, in his 1978 book *Striper: A Story of Fish and Man,* also discusses aspects of the background and history of the East End baymen, principally the ocean haul seiners. Both Matthiessen and Cole actually were baymen and fished on the East End, principally on the South Fork in the waters of East Hampton Town. They fished during the 1950s with the generation of baymen who are the parents and grandparents of some of those with whom I fished and write about here. My experiences were not as a wage-earning and "producing" bayman, as were Matthiessen and Cole, but as a marine biologist studying the marine environs and having the privilege of working beside many wonderful baymen, and other people on Long Island, principally in the 1970s and a bit in the 1980s.

Introduction

On August 9, 2007, the *East Hampton Star* contained an obituary of bayman Calvin Lester. He died of cancer at age 54. I knew Calvin as a young vigorous bayman in the 1970s who worked hard and earned the respect of the other baymen with whom he associated. I did not know Calvin well, but I was influenced by his vigor and his selflessness which I write about in chapter 2. I completed the first good draft of my manuscript, the one I sent to Byron Young and Ed Sherrill for review, before that August, 2007 obit on Calvin. When I opened The *Star* and saw the photo of Calvin on the obituary page, my heart just sank. He was among the last of the true East End baymen. A piece of the old East End passed with Calvin, I think, and I wept for both. I went back to my stories in chapter 2 that included Calvin and thought about revising them to indicate his passing. I decided not to, and I leave him very much alive here, as I remember him.

My story of people, community, and the environment on the East End in this book begins with a reflection from a visit I made there with my young family in 1986. It was a wonderful visit and allowed me to introduce my children to my East End friends. It also was an eye-opening moment during which I realized first hand, and for the first time, that the East End and its traditional fishing community were changing. The vigor of that community that I observed, and was part of, just 10–15 years earlier was waning. In the '70s, the vigor of the fishing community as I observed it was centered around: a robust local community of people, traditional fishermen and their families, who had been fishing on the East End for many generations; an ample and available natural supply of fish and shellfish resources; an active local Town Baymen's Association and a newly formed fishermen's seafood cooperative; cooperation among fishermen and scientists to study and conserve the fishery resources; and involvement of fishermen and some fishing organizations in local community affairs and government.

On the East End

Restoration and Wholeness. Concord Point Light sits watch at the head of Chesapeake Bay, where the Susquehanna River meets the Bay at the town of Havre de Grace. I frequently stop and rest at Concord Point during my treks from Maryland to points north. I found the Light in 1980 and have watched as the Light and its keeper's house have been restored and opened as historic public treasures. During the time of that restoration process, the coastal striped bass fishery was closed so that the stock could be rebuilt as a public treasure. Since its erection in 1827, Concord Point Light has watched over the interaction of the River and the Bay and the myriad anadromous striped bass that have passed by en route to and from the spawning grounds there. Both the coastal striped bass stock and Concord Point Light now are restored and reopened. These important actions occurred because of people working together to steward their environmental commons.

The East End landscape was changing. It was burgeoning with new homes, large ones, many as second homes for non-residents. The cost of living was skyrocketing, leaving the local people in its wake. The marine and bay waters were changing, the fisheries resources and their conservation management were changing, and so too were the people who relied on them. Chapter 5 is my reflection on all of

Introduction

Respect. During my family's return trip to the East End in 1986 I showed my daughters how to fish for snapper bluefish. My younger daughter proudly displays her catch, still on the hook, just removed from Accabonac Creek at Louse Point on Gardiner's Bay. Fishing is a good way to teach children about the relationship between people and the environment, and about the life cycle of marine animals and how to treat them humanely. It is an opportunity to teach about conservation, the rules that apply, why there are rules at all, and why just obeying the rules is not enough to steward the environment..

that. Several local publications that describe the East End's recent deteriorating environment and water quality, and which offer some societal actions to reverse them, are discussed. It pains me greatly to think that I may have chosen the correct subtitle for this book and the title for chapter 5, which relates the 1970s with the years since.

Finally, in chapter 5 and throughout this story, I offer many environmental observations, as well as what may be some environmental stewardship truths and principles. These truths seem to me to be universal ones for care and stewardship of both people and the environment of the East End, especially as related to fishers and their fishery resources. I offer these out of my profound love for that place and its people. One of these environmental stewardship truths is that the healing and wholeness of the people must precede the healing and wholeness of the environment and the natural resources on which the people depend. Only when people—all the people of the

East End—are "in community" with each other, can they effectively work together to steward the things they hold in common, such as the environment and its natural resources.

The East End's citizens need to strengthen their personal ethical relationships with each other and with the landscape and the sea. Conservation laws and regulations, that govern the people's environmental behavior, offer only a minimum level of environmental protection. Just obeying the law is not enough. The people must go beyond the laws, with voluntary and personal ethical actions toward the environment, in order to fully steward and protect it.

Laws and regulations for protection of the environment also need to consider the human element and not just the natural element. Conservation laws need to be designed and enforced by government in ways that build human community, and not degrade it, while the environment is being nurtured and protected. While the laws are building, or rebuilding, the integrity of the environment, they need to support and enable the human community.

Only a "whole" people will work together altruistically and will affect positively the wholeness of the environment. People who live by the conservation laws and sacrifice for environmental healing and wholeness should be able to reap the rewards of a rebuilt, revitalized, or renewed environment and its natural resources. Sacrifice for environmental healing should lead to a strengthened human community, as well as sustainable natural communities. All the people who are connected in any way with the East End and its environment are stakeholders in its present and its future. All of these interested and affected people must come together as an extended community, working together altruistically, in order to affect beneficially the destiny of the East End. Our destinies are all entwined and all are one.

Clarence Hickey
Rockville, Maryland
April, 2015

1

Another Year

"You guys are going to **MONTAUK** for your summer vacation? Stay **OUTA** the water!" was the advice given by fellow Marylanders. "OK, I won't swim 25 miles offshore or hang around with any dead whales," I assured them. Their advice and my response were triggered by some widespread newspaper and TV press reports in the summer of 1986 about a 3,450 pound great white shark landed on Montauk on August 7 by the "Monster Man," Captain Frank Mundus, and his shark fishing boat *Cricket*. The movie "Jaws," based on Peter Benchley's book, had the entire East Coast uneasy about swimming in the ocean. The movie was released in June 1975 when I still was on the East End, but its influence lasted long after the late '70s. The coastal town setting in the movie appeared to be a small town on Long Island and the movie's shark fisherman, Quint, was very much like Montauk's Monster Man. Even with the story of "Jaws" set on Long Island, I very much looked forward to once again seeing and reuniting with my old friend Montauk and the East End of Long Island. Actually, I refused to see the movie in the theater in the '70s, because it seemed to contribute to an anti-shark hysteria that worked against an understanding of sharks and their place as top predators in the ocean.

Places can become your friend if you let them, and they can embrace, comfort, and nurture you with their very being. The East End is one such place in my life. During that week in the summer of 1986, my wife Mary and I took our two young daughters to Amagansett, a village on the East End in the Town of East Hampton. There we would reunite with old friends and that rural seacoast landscape we missed so much since moving to Maryland in 1976. Our week there that year was wonderful and nostalgic, happy and sad. Sad, because things were different that year, and not like they were when we lived there just ten years earlier.

The marine environment seemed a bit worn out and tired. And our commercial fishing baymen friends and their families seemed discouraged and melancholy. 1986 also was the year following the legal closure of commercial fishing for striped bass in New York State. The closure, that would remain in place for five years, was enacted due to a reduced East Coast striped bass population and to pollution in the Hudson River that rendered some bass unfit for consumption. I had been very involved researching the biology of striped bass, with the assistance of many East End baymen, in the early 1970s. Striped bass was a mainstay of the fishery then and its closure had hit the local fishing community especially hard. Mary and I reflected on all of this as we drove home to Maryland at the end of our week.

For those unfamiliar with the East End, it is that area of Long Island comprising the five eastern-most towns of Shelter Island, Riverhead, Southold, Southampton, and East Hampton. The East End geographically is about 100 miles east of New York City and is divided by the Peconic Bay system into two arms, referred to locally as the North and South Forks. The southern arm from Southampton

Another Year

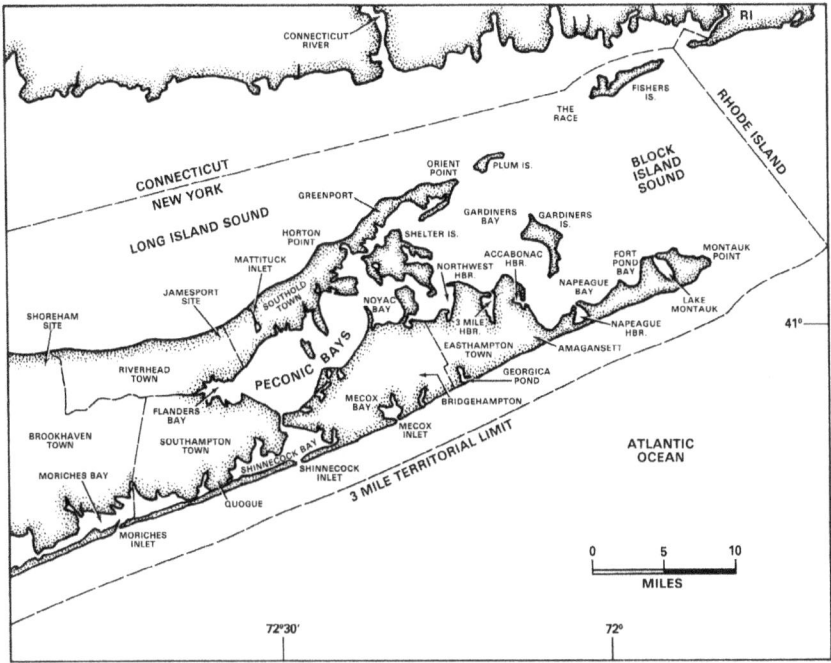

The East End. This is a chart of Long Island's East End showing the South Fork from Southampton to Montauk, and the North Fork from Riverhead to Orient Point. I lived in Amagansett near Accabonac Harbor (Bonac Creek). Those baymen who fished "up bay" and in the estuaries did so mainly between the North and South Forks, in Northwest Harbor, Gardiner's Bay, and in the Peconic Bays. The East Hampton Town ocean haul seiners operated along the "back side," the beaches between Amagansett and Montauk. Jimmy Lester's pound nets were in Fort Pond Bay, near the easternmost tip of the South Fork.

to Montauk (pronounced as "mun-TAWK" by the locals) is referred to as the "South Fork." The South Fork residents of Amagansett and Springs in East Hampton Town, especially those with roots several generations old, are often referred to as "Bonackers." The name originally applied to those who lived in that part of town near the salt marshes of Accabonac Creek (or "Bonac" Creek), which supplied much of their food and economic needs. Bonac Creek is an estuary on Gardiner's Bay on the South Fork. The association between

Bonackers and the water is as old as the East End settlements themselves, dating back to the mid-seventeenth century. The respect of and need for the water and its bounties remain still.

I've been told by friends that I have "Bonac in my blood." Yes, it's true. Ever since living, working, playing, and worshipping there in the 1970s, the East End has been in my blood. The salt water that used to be in my marine biologist veins now is much less saline, but the East End still flows within me with each heartbeat. It has influenced everything I have thought and done professionally and environmentally. Not a day goes by that I don't think about and remember the landscape and people there. In my youth I was a "summer person," loving the warm summer months, especially the beaches of the East Coast.

The East End converted me to a winter person who loved its quiet and the solitude of being the only one on the beach. I still subscribe to and read the local newspaper, the *East Hampton Star*. I would be lost and alone without it. Yes, these days, I usually open *The Star* first to the obituaries where I too often see accounts of the lives of people I knew or knew of. I clip those I knew. I've seen many baymen and their relatives in recent years. That always makes me reflective of my years on the East End when I was a fishery researcher working with live fish and lively fishermen. I worked beside several baymen who taught me about living by and from the sea.

A Nostalgic Trip Home

We have been fortunate in returning to the East End every few years to be with good old friends and to reacquaint with the land and water. We were glad to return when our children were young and introduce them to those same good friends, both human and otherwise in 1986, a visit that stands out in my memory for what we learned that year about a changing landscape and people. We were all packed and ready to head back home after that summer's week. Packing didn't

Another Year

take long. We had it down to an art form, Mary and I. But leaving Amagansett that year was especially hard, harder than in other years. One week in Bonac, during mid-August, with our friends, didn't seem like enough that year, "Have your children (ages six and eight then) enjoyed themselves? Do they like coming here?" a friend asked. They did like it, and sensed there's something special about coming here, about being here, about those friends. Like the "something special" about Grandma and Grandpa's in New Jersey. The feeling we gave it, they sensed. So, we said our good-byes and headed out. Schellinger Road to Oak Lane, then west on Montauk Highway. Maryland bound.

As we approached the Long Island Dwarf Pine Barrens, I recalled Montauk's Hither Woods and the evidence of the great forest fire of earlier in that year of 1986. En route to Montauk Harbor early one morning with bayman friends Jimmy and Sandy Lester, we had driven through Hither Woods and I saw where the fire had jumped the highway. The trees were barren, except for tufts of green atop some, and the woods resembled winter. It was reminiscent, also, of the damage done by gypsy moths to the oak forests near our home in Springs during the 1970s. I could see deep into the woods through the trees. The understory was green, however, and thick. Nature's rebuilding had begun. We heard of accounts of the 1986 fire from Alan Steil, a friend and Montauk fireman. His wife, Celeste, spent the night comforting their young children at the home of a friend. For several days thereafter, the sound of a fire siren brought the children to Mom's arms.

There also was other evidence of an unusual year we observed during that week of vacation. The ocean was calm most days, with northerly winds kicking up the bay waters, but calming the ocean back-side. The ocean beach at Amagansett, however, had a winter-berm-look to it. Not the wide summer beach with gentle slope and small, almost imperceptible, sand bar offshore. The berm was narrow, and cut deeply at the water's edge, to form a cliff of sand 3–4 feet high. We could jump off the berm, or slide down (as kids and dads are wont to do), to the beach face, where gentle waves were leaving swash marks of sand, redepositing it from a large and obvious bar a few hundred yards offshore. That was evidence, I assumed, of storms that had passed through during early August. It did not deter us from enjoying the summer sun and surf, however. After clinging close to Dad for some time, Leigh Anne (our eight-year-old) managed to body surf her first wave ashore. Something I did profusely at the Jersey shore during the 1960s and at Ditch Plain on Montauk during the 1970s.

Sun and swimming we found also in Gardiner's Bay at Louse Point. There were friendly people along the beach, enjoying the quiet, the water, the warmth. Windsurfers, students and instructors, were busy hotdogging on the westerly winds. It looked like fun. An elderly couple was having trouble discerning Montauk from Gardiner's Island across the water, and the Montauk water tower from Montauk Lighthouse way off in the distance. So, I set them straight and, for a moment, felt like the Springs resident I once was, who lived and breathed as many moments as possible at Louse Point and Bonac Creek. Louse Point was a friend who consoled me, comforted me, informed and educated me. I still can smell the wind across her natural salt marsh.

The inside beach at Louse Point was busy, as well. Some people were swimming in the channel right near the signs stating East Hampton Town's position on not doing so. That made it very difficult (impossible, actually) for me to fish there with my daughters, so we moved out onto the sand spit. There, anglers of all ages were lined up along the shore in pursuit of snappers, the young and immature bluefish. That scene was reminiscent of the 1970s Montauk surf casters, shoulder-to-shoulder, at North Bar, seeking the ever elusive striped bass. West winds made it tough casting at Louse Point that day, but alas, our younger daughter Beth was tougher. She made several fine casts, but those snappers were a cast-and-a-half away. (She fishes like her dad sometimes.)

Just holding the fishing rod, however, always seemed to clear my mind of cobwebs and work-related drivel. When a lad to my left cast to starboard, instead of ahead, and landed his lure and sinker on my shoulder, it was time to leave. Now, kids will do that accidentally, just as dads will put their casts into the trees or watch as the line snaps and the gear makes a beautiful cast-and-a-half right into the boiling school of fish. But, Beth finally did hook a nice snapper and bring it in, which prompted several young boys to run to our fishing location and crowd us out. So, around the spit we went to comb the beach for summer treasures - shells, crab carapaces, horseshoe crab molts, smooth surf-worn pebbles, and seaweeds. There always was a nice variety along the Gardiner's Bay beaches. The shells made for fun special-time projects with the girls during the following winter.

Something's Wrong with the Water

Those thoughts left me as we drove west and crossed the Shinnecock Canal, where I strained quickly to see north and south, the bay and the marinas. The previous year of 1985, on our way home (also in mid-August), we stopped for refreshment at a restaurant on the canal. The water was dark brown from the "brown tide" algae bloom that appeared that year. During this year's visit, the East End waters I saw looked normal. Apparently the bloom had decreased significantly and earlier than in 1985, but its effects had not. I recall talking with several friends about the brown tide, and their observations. One marine scientist friend gave me his theory of climate and rainfall variations that contributed to the bloom, and told me that both Narragansett Bay, RI, and Barnegat Bay, NJ, had experienced similar problems that year. Bayman friend Jimmy Lester expressed frustration and concern with declining water quality and poor spring and summer harvests in the East End bays. "Something's wrong with the water," he added, in a tone reminiscent of that expressed by Chesapeake Bay watermen in William Warner's book *Beautiful Swimmers*: "You look hard at the water and sometimes it seems like it's getting a little old and tired, a little messy. Simple as that, if anyone cares to notice." That's kind of how Jimmy explained it to me that year. But fishing around the East End seemed to be more or less normal for mid-summer in 1986, at least in the open waters off East Hampton Town. There were fluke and bluefish. Plenty of snappers, mostly small. A few draggers working the backside. Reports of tuna, billfish, and sharks offshore.

Shoreward, things were very different in 1986. I visited Montauk Harbor with Jimmy and Sandy, while Jimmy worked on his fishing boat *Tern*. I chanced to meet some baymen I knew and listened in on their conversation. Two fishermen, Richard Lester and Pete Kromer, were ocean haul-seiners in former times, and might do so again, I suspected, if the new conservation laws prohibiting the harvest of striped bass then were relaxed at some point in the future. Richard had a boat and was doing some lobstering, along with many others, I guessed. Block Island Sound between Montauk Harbor and Fort Pond Bay was as congested that year with lobster pot buoys as was Amagansett with traffic on a summer Saturday morning. Pete was en route to a fillet house to perform one of those work tasks that baymen were especially good at. Both men were adapting to changing times. Flexibility among several fisheries and among fishery or water-related work is a hallmark, a must, of a true bayman. The ability to change from this species to that, from this gear to that, from this activity to that, quickly and relatively inexpensively, had permitted the survival of the baymen's way of life.

That way of life now appeared to be changing due to degradation of the environmental quality of the bays, to reduced abundance of harvestable fishes and shellfishes, and to conservation regulations that curtailed the fishing for some species. Dick Stern also passed by and joined in the conversation. He was a big strapping guy, deep voice, retired draggerman. Very salty. The mood of the group was up and down. Discussion of what's running and where, boat repairs and parts, who's doing what. I saw a few smiles, and a general concerned manner, frustration and disappointment. While talking or listening, each would glance at the other, then look off toward the harbor. Jimmy kept busy with maintenance jobs on *Tern*. I watched and listened. Most of the former ocean haul seiners were working in some fishing-related activities, Sandy told me.

I felt a bit melancholy after listening to that discussion among the baymen. I was a member of the East Hampton Town Baymen's Association when I lived in Amagansett in the early 1970s and I recall the vigor, enthusiasm, and busyness among the men, their families, and the fishing community then. They were all working, the fishes and shellfishes were plentiful, the waters relatively clean and productive. The 1985 brown tide algae bloom had taken a heavy toll on the shellfishes of the bays and estuaries, especially the bay scallop. The coastal striped bass population was so low in abundance that the harvest had been totally closed in 1985 to both commercial and recreational fisheries along the entire Mid-Atlantic Coast. So, the bays and the ocean backside, where baymen have fished for generations, were producing fewer harvests and less income, and affecting the lives and very being of the people. Some of the traditional diversity of the East End's harvestable species seemed to be in decline. And the cultural identity of the baymen's community seemed in question when they could not fish for traditional species and in traditional ways. I did see Calvin Lester's fishing crew heading out from Amagansett once or twice during that week of 1986, with an ocean dory in tow, in pursuit of bluefish I guessed. As I watched his truck and dory head east on Montauk Highway through the usual summer traffic, I realized (or admitted to myself) for the first time that the traditional commercial fishing community was becoming a decreasingly smaller part of what was happening in East Hampton Town. It had always been a large part for me.

Soon after we left town that August of 1986, there was a big bash celebrating the publication of Peter Matthiessen's new book *Men's Lives*. I would like to have been there for the celebration, but we had to get back home. I did get a copy, and some other local books for winter reading. *Men's Lives* documented in some detail what I had observed that same year about the disillusioned baymen and a declining vigor of the fishing community.

Those winter reading books were tucked away in the spare tire boot of my station wagon. The spare was tied to the roof rack. I always envisioned a flat tire on the Jersey Turnpike, and having to unload the wagon to get the spare, so it was on the roof and easily accessible. In southern New Jersey along the turnpike there is a restaurant and inn with a Dutch-looking windmill facing the highway. It always reminded me of East Hampton's Hook Mill, and the sights and happenings of our week in East Hampton with our kids and our friends.

During that week in the summer 1986, we visited "Home Sweet Home," had dinner with friends, enjoyed Sedutto's ice cream, and chewed on penny gum balls. We took a drive through Georgica and took in a pool party with friends. A visit to *The Star* office was especially nice and informative. I had written several articles for *The Star*, and the staff I knew there gave my children a nice tour behind the scenes. We saw a fox cross the road while driving through the woods in northwest part of town. Ate plenty of fresh fluke and lobster. Enjoyed a sunset dinner overlooking Three Mile Harbor with old friends Georgeanne and Carl. A stop at Marty's Deli in Springs to say hi. A day on the water fishing with Jimmy. One whale of a reunion party with some folks we haven't seen in more than ten years, many of them former employees of the Ocean Science Lab on Montauk. And a visit to the beach at Ditch Plain on Montauk to hear the ocean growl.

Watch and Listen. A 1971 view of the coastal bluffs at Ditch Plain on the ocean side of Montauk, where land, sea, and atmosphere intersect. Montauk is part of the terminal moraine from the last glacial advance and retreat. As the weather and the sea erode these bluffs, rocks and boulders are freed and drop to the beach. The ocean wave action then pounds, churns, and grinds them into pebbles, gravel, and coarse beach sand.

Ditch Plain is a special and unique place where an astute observer can hear the ocean growl. The growl is the soothing, yet eerie sound of surf-worn rocks colliding with each other as they move up and down the beach face with each wave. It is said that old salts and experienced surfers can tell the condition of the sea on a pitch-black night by just the sound of the growl. Even when you are standing among the rocks on this beach, the growl is not obvious. Often it is muffled by the sound of the crashing surf and the wind.

You must put everything else out of your mind, then watch and listen. It is like finding your first four-leafed clover. You look and look and see none, but once you find your first one, many abound. When you first recognize the growl, it will give you shivers, as it does me, remembering and writing this. Places like Ditch Plain, where the ocean growls, are like those Irish "thin places" where the real and natural meet the spiritual. There is a very spiritual quality in being open to the workings, the whims, and the moods of the sea. Watch, and listen.

Well, we made it to the Delaware Memorial Bridge and I strained to see the water, the ships of Delaware Bay. It is a very high bridge and I watched the gulls soar at eye level while atop it. I heard a talking gull once, while fishing with Jimmy. Honest. Heading south, we crossed the Susquehanna River on I-95 in Maryland. Yes, I strained again for views of the water. On a clear day, Conowingo Dam is visible upstream, and Chesapeake Bay at Havre de Grace downstream. That drive home in 1986 was a long and contemplative one during which we a reflected on our visit. It brought back all those wonderful memories of our life on the East End and my working with the baymen. I reflected on the Baymen's Association and their meetings in the Town Marine Museum, on tagging striped bass on the ocean beaches with the haul seiners, on all the fishes I encountered on Long Island Sound, and my adventures at sea. I especially reflected on fishing with Jimmy Lester on Montauk's Fort Pond Bay. But things were different in on the East End in 1986 and it troubled me.

We drove through Baltimore (pronounced "BALL-uh-mer" by the natives) and the new Fort McHenry Tunnel. One more hour south to home in Rockville. 348 miles. Another year.

2

Of Baymen and Striped Bass

Being associated with striped bass during the early and mid-1970s was exciting. The coastal stock was very abundant and many fishermen were in pursuit. The ever elusive striped bass was the most sought after of marine fishes by New York's recreational and commercial fishermen, and was the bellwether of the robustness of the local fishing communities. The abundance and availability of striped bass also suggested the integrity of the marine environment that produced it and that supported the fisheries. During the period from late the 1950s through the early 1970s, the Chesapeake Bay striped bass spawning and nursery grounds had been working overtime. They produced large year classes of young fish, so that the northeast coastal migratory stock of bass was abundant and dominated overwhelmingly by striped bass spawned in the Chesapeake. The coastal fisheries also contained bass spawned in the Hudson River, as well as bass from Delaware Bay and North Carolina, but their proportionate numbers were much less than those from Maryland and Virginia waters of the Chesapeake at that time.

Striped Bass and Mae West

In the spring of 1972, the Montauk Ocean Science Lab's chief fishery scientist, Dr. Herb Austin, began a study of the movements and migrations of striped bass caught on the South Fork by local baymen. Herb and his staff, myself included, accompanied bayman Jimmy Lester while he tended his pound nets in Fort Pond Bay on Montauk. Jimmy's pound nets, or fish traps as the baymen called them, were stationary nets just a few hundred yards to the west of the Lab on the southern shore of the Bay. When Jimmy caught striped bass, he would sort out the "keepers" for market. They were fish 16" in length or longer, the minimum legal length requirement for keeper striped bass by the State of New York. We would sort out the undersized bass, the "shorts," that Jimmy would release unharmed. They would be next year's catch and harvest.

We measured each short fish and removed some scale samples to determination the age of each fish. Striped bass scales have annual rings, much as trees do, that enabled us to count the rings and thus age each fish. Those short fish predominantly were two years of age, with some three-year-olds mixed in. We then applied small red plastic tags to the short fish and released them alive back into Fort Pond Bay. The tags were numbered and printed with "Return to NYOSL Montauk NY 11954," so that when a fisherman caught the tagged bass they could return the tag along with some information on when and where the bass was caught, and hopefully the length of the bass they caught.

Montauk Lab Fishery Scientists. The author (at right) and two colleagues at the New York Ocean Science Laboratory, Montauk, in 1973. At left is Richard A. Amish, a graduate of the marine science program at Southampton College of Long Island University. Rick and I did a lot of field sampling together and authored a brief paper on striped bass. In the center of things here, as he was at the Lab, is Dr. Herbert M. Austin, who was the fisheries department head. Herb had made the first contact with bayman Jimmy Lester in 1971 when Jimmy was tending his pound nets in Fort Pond Bay, just west of the Lab site. Herb and Jimmy began what was a productive relationship between the Lab scientists and local baymen for the study of local fishes.

The tags that were returned to us by fishermen, from those bass we released into Fort Pond Bay in the spring of 1972, reflected the dominance of the Chesapeake stock of striped bass in the New York fishery then. Sixty-three percent of the returns of two year old bass we tagged during the spring of 1972 came back from the Chesapeake Bay area in the winter and spring the following year, 1973. And during that time of freedom between being tagged on Montauk and caught in the Chesapeake (an average time of 326 days), those bass grew on the average from 10.2 inches to 16.5 inches in length, an increase of greater than 60 percent between their second and third years of life. Now who wouldn't marvel at such an animal! Beautiful. Spirited. Coastal traveler, winters in the Chesapeake, summers in the Hamptons and New England. Very hardy with a marvelous rate of growth. And able to stir the mind, soul, and virility of countless recreational fishermen in a dozen eastern coastal states, while supporting the centuries old traditions of East End baymen. Eat your heart out, Mae West!

Listening

With those fish tagging studies on Montauk in 1972, I began a long and wonderful friendship with bayman Jimmy Lester. We both worked on Montauk and lived in Amagansett, a small East End village several miles west of Montauk. It was in Amagansett that I first met the local fisherman and where I would participate with them in many local fisheries matters. After moving to Amagansett in 1970, my wife and I joined the Amagansett Presbyterian Church where we both taught Sunday School and where I served as an Elder from 1972–1975. It was there that I met Elder and fisherman Norman Edwards, who was captain of a menhaden fishing boat that was part of a company fleet based in Port Monmouth, New Jersey. During the fishing season, Norman would shuttle back and forth between Amagansett and Port Monmouth on a company airplane. Norman was an 11th generation member of a family of fisherman and farmers with roots going back to 1652 in Amagansett. He was a friendly man, very youthful looking in his 50s, with a great smile and expressive eyes. I would see Norman in church on Sunday mornings and we would exchange information on his fishing and my work at the Lab. He would ask me questions on menhaden biology and behavior, most of which he could answer himself. His years of fishing, and the generations of fishermen in his family, had given him much knowledge beyond my "book learning." It may have been those brief moments talking with Norman that helped me to first realize that the best way to talk with a commercial fisherman was to listen, and not to expound on the virtues of science.

I also learned not to dwell on those 50-cent words that scientists love to utter. Words like *Brevoortia tyrannus*, the biological genus and species names for the menhaden. Why, "menhaden" wasn't even the name of the fish in local East End fishing circles; it was "bunker" or "mossbunker." Oh, my. Another local bay fish, the longhorn sculpin (more properly *Myoxocephalus octodecimspinosus*), was the "hackle-head" or "horned toad." Windowpane flounders were "daylights" and northern puffers were "blow-toads." Sea ravens were "red sculpins" and blue runners were "yellow jacks." Cut me a break, here! And the Atlantic Ocean between Amagansett and Montauk, where many of these fishes were caught, was the "Backside." The backside of what, I wondered. And many local baymen worked "up bay" in East Hampton Town waters, wherever that was.

There were many baymen of the Lester family in Amagansett. The Lesters were a fishing family whose ancestors had been fishing East End waters for generations, centuries. That seemed easy enough, but they appeared to live in what seemed like clans or enclaves tucked away in the local villages and hamlets. There were "Posey" Lesters from Poseyville in Amagansett, which wasn't on any map I had. And there were "Pantigo" Lesters from East Hampton, and "Round Swamp" Lesters from somewhere. I had a lot to learn as a new East Ender.

One of my good friends and colleagues at the Lab on Montauk was Lab staff photographer Carl Mamay. Carl lived in the wooded section north of Amagansett Village called The Springs next to a bayman named Tom Lester. Yes, a Round-Swamper from near Three Mile Harbor. Tom was a large strong man who fished up bay, which

I learned was in the Northwest Harbor area of East Hampton, which faced northerly into that bay area between the North and South Forks. He fished pound nets during the spring-through-fall fishing season. He and also fished for flounders by fyke-net, a small stationary and submerged net used in shallow water to trap and catch fishes, and sometimes turtles, as they move about.

The fyke-net, or fish fyke, is used during late winter for flounder in the shallow bays and harbors when the fish move into those areas to spawn. After spawning is complete, they begin to feed voraciously and become the quarry of sport fishermen, during April and May. Tom also tonged for clams, fished for scallops by dredge during the fall, and ice-fished during the dead of winter when the bays froze over. Tom was a true bayman in the oldest and best sense of that fishing tradition. East End baymen were individuals and opportunist fishermen who worked by the tides and the seasons of the year. The seasons were determined by which fish species were running or by which shellfish were legally in season for harvest. Baymen also made their own twine or fishing nets and even built their own small boats for use on the bays. One winter, Tom was building a large seine net in his living room for use the next spring. The net was strung all around and encompassed the entire space. When asked how long the net was, Tom answered, "Fifty-six living rooms."

Tom had a Chesapeake retriever, a great dog named Sally, that he trained to retrieve ducks from the bays during hunting season. Many baymen took along a shotgun in their boats when scalloping or clamming in the winter, just in case an opportunity presented itself for a duck or goose dinner. Tom trained Sally to follow his hand signals from the boat, or while he was standing on the shore, after a bird was down in the water. When Sally was swimming after a downed bird, if she got confused and lost track of just where the bird lay on the water, she would turn and look back at Tom who would point an arm right, left, or straight ahead. Sally would swim in the direction Tom indicated and find the bird every time.

Of Baymen and Striped Bass

Tom brought unusual fishes he caught in his pound nets in Northwest Creek (yes, up bay) to the Lab for identification. Two of his fish captures were "firsts," and we Lab scientists wrote about them. Herb Austin identified an adult rhomboid mojarra (yes, *Diapterus rhombeus*) Tom caught in 1971. It was the first and only record of that fish species from U.S. mainland waters, which Austin published in the journal *Chesapeake Science* in 1973. When he was at the University of Puerto Rico, Austin had studied rhomboid mojarras which are native to Caribbean and South American waters. Tom's mainland capture thus was a real find. Tom also caught a gizzard shad, a member of the herring family, in 1974. It was the first record of the species from Long Island waters. Tom and I published this find in the *New York Fish and Game Journal* in 1976.

A few years later, Tom's pound net fishing partner was bayman Bradley Loewen, Tom's nephew. In 1974, Brad called me about a greater amberjack (*Seriola dumerili*) he caught in his pound net in Gardiner's Bay near Three Mile Harbor. It was a beautiful and powerful looking fish, 52 inches long weighing 58 pounds. It was the first conclusive record of the greater amberjack from New York marine waters. While a few specimens have been caught since then, I believe that Brad's fish still is the largest on record for that species in New York waters. Brad and I wrote a brief paper on his catch and published it in the *New York Fish and Game Journal* in 1976. The *Fish and Game Journal* always was interested in documenting the diversity of fish fauna in New York's waters and it was a great local way to do so that I used frequently. I was fortunate to have been able to co-author papers in the *Fish and Game Journal* with baymen Tom Lester and Brad Loewen, both of whom were civic minded people. Brad, like his uncle Tom, was involved as a leader in the East Hampton Town Baymen's Association. More recently, Brad was elected to the office of East Hampton Town Trustee.

Those three articles used photos of the fishes taken by Carl Mamay, as did many of the scientific articles I published in journals and magazines. Carl was an expert photographer, and an even better dark room technician. He could photograph a dead fish, or other marine life, and make them look alive and kicking in his photos. Carl came to know Tom Lester pretty well, since they were neighbors. Carl also was a gook listener and the two of them could talk for hours about fishing and the business of the Baymen's Association.

Carl also was an expert hook-and-line fisher, with many stories to tell. He could spin a good fishing yarn, like the time one early spring morning, on the Lab dock in Fort Pond Bay, when two young women college interns at the Lab were fishing and asked Carl if the flounders had stopped spawning and were biting yet. "No," he explained in his usual soft demeanor, "they're still fykin'." Not until they had blushed and hurried away, did Carl realize that the girls had misunderstood. The baymen smiled, as do I in recalling that. Such long talks, and the trading of stories, usually took place in their kitchens, around the table, for hours. Such was the East End custom. In the local homes, you always entered through the back door or kitchen door, never through the front door. In some homes, the front door wasn't even usable since there was furniture right up against it.

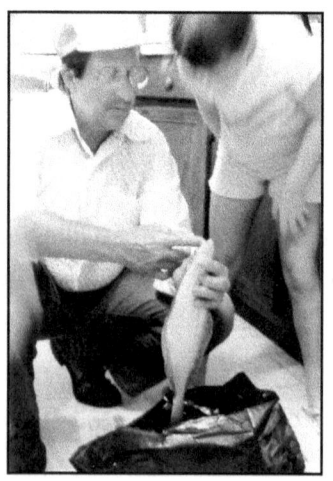

Photographer, Fisher, and Bayman. Colleague Carl Mamay. Ever the teacher and mentor, Carl Mamay is explaining to my elder daughter the ins and outs of a fluke, or summer flounder, during one of our visits to the East End in the 1980s. After a successful harvest of fluke, Carl was making ready to cook them up. He loved to fish and was a master caster. Carl made most of his own fishing rods and had many different kinds for all manner of fishing. He liked to talk fishing and was equally good at the real thing from shore or boat.

Diversity and Fun. My photographer friend Carl Mamay took this photo of a variety of sea stars that were caught bottom trawling aboard R/V *Albatross IV* at various ocean locations in 1974. I brought back some representative samples of oceanic marine life for the scientists at the Ocean Science Lab on Montauk. Carl arranged these starfish specimens, set the lighting, and provided a deep-sea blue background. What I don't know to this day is whether Carl intended to make the starfishes appear to be in motion, but they look to me like dancers.

The Baymen's Association

The East Hampton Town Baymen's Association was the local organization of commercial fishermen, most of whom were inshore fishers, like Tom. The Association had begun in the late 1950s from a need recognized by several baymen, who today are seen as icons of the local fishing industry—Milt Miller, William Havens, Francis Lester, and Billy Lester (Jimmy's father). The association was made up trap net fishermen, haul seiners, scallopers, clammers, pin hookers, gill netters, long-liners, a few draggermen (trawler fishermen) from Montauk, and others. It was dedicated to protecting the environmental quality of the marine waters, to promoting the welfare of the fishing industry, and to representing the fishermen's interests before local government, the county legislature, and even the State Assembly in Albany. Conservation was a keen interest, since livelihoods depended on clean waters and dependable fish stocks.

In 1974, the Association was having a membership drive, and Tom Lester was on the membership committee. Tom was a civic minded person, served several terms as Town Trustee, and was very concerned about the business of the Baymen's Association. He attended every meeting, sat in the front row taking up three seats, and usually spoke his mind and spoke it well. Tom's wife Cathy also was civic minded. She was a baywoman at heart and passionate about fishing and the environment. Cathy was a member of the town planning board, then the town board, and finally she served as East Hampton Town Supervisor. Tom and Cathy Lester were citizens for all seasons.

I came to know Tom through Carl. The Association was interested in recruiting non-fishermen members who were interested in the same conservation issues, so when Tom called me about membership, I accepted. Carl and I joined at the same time. Not all of the baymen were so eager to accept Lab staff and scientists into their ranks, however. Many fishermen had a distrust of scientists, especially those who want to manage the fisheries. Fishery management to the baymen meant new rules, fishing constraints, and legislative battles. One bayman, a trawler captain from Montauk, asked me if I thought that any of the fishery science work I did at the Lab would ever help him to catch more fish. "Probably not," I admitted, "and I will learn more from you than you will learn from me." I had learned from Norman, Tom, and Jimmy to be a good listener and not to take any such comments personally. Carl's and my willingness to participate with the Association was accepted with cautious optimism. We faithfully attended the evening monthly Association meetings held in the East Hampton Town Marine Museum on Bluff Road, in Amagansett. We went on our own time and were careful not to give the impression that we represented the Lab. We represented ourselves. The relationship proved to be good for our friendships with the fishermen and for our work at the Lab by the teaching and learning we were afforded. It also contributed to the trust eventually built among many of the fishermen and us.

Many of the fishermen's wives were involved with the Baymen's Association Auxiliary, and were referred to, affectionately, as the "Bayladies." The wives frequently fished with their husbands and many of them also managed the record books and finances for their baymen husbands. Some daughters also fished with their fathers. Author Sandra Weiner wrote about one such young lady, Christine Vorpahl, in her 1977 book *I Want to be a Fisherman*. Christine was 11 years old and fished with her bayman father Stuart Vorpahl, Jr. The Vorpahls were a several-generations-old East End fishing family. Stuart was intelligent, well spoken, and especially civic minded. He was concerned about the local fishing industry, the environment of the bays and estuaries, and he frequently spoke with local government about these. Stuart was a good role model and teacher for young Christine.

Jimmy's wife, Kathi, also was very involved in the workings of the Baymen's Association and the bayladies. Kathi took on the task of helping to develop and edit a new newsletter for the Baymen's Association in the early 1970s. She was very organized, and a good writer and artist. Carl and I participated in the planning of the newsletter and sat on one of the Association's committees with a few fishermen. Carl had a long career involvement with public affairs and public information and he suggested that the newsletter needed to have a nice logo identifying it. A logo was developed showing some fish, a net, and the name of the Baymen's Association. Volume I of *The Baymen's Newsletter* appeared in June 1974 and had a nice lead story on ocean haul seining. It was replete with articles written by Kathi as well as her artwork. Over time, I contributed many brief articles and notes to the *Newsletter* on my fishery biology work, and

The Bayladies. The Baymen's Association Ladies Auxiliary was an active organization composed mostly of women related to the baymen, but like the Baymen's Association itself, membership was open to anyone interested in the Association and its purposes. My wife Mary participated. For several years in the 1970s, the "bayladies," as they were affectionately known, awarded $500 scholarships to local high-school graduates for college studies in natural resources and the environment. Here, two of the bayladies are selling cakes, crafts, and gifts in the Co-op seafood shop to support the scholarship program. The Co-op, even in its brief existence, stands out in my mind as an example of the vigor of the fishing community and many of the baymen of East Hampton Town in the 1970s.

especially on the unusual fishes that came to me from many of the baymen. New York State Department of Environmental Conservation biologist Byron Young also contributed articles to the *Newsletter*. I especially liked the *Newsletter's* interviews with the elder baymen and their discussion of historical fishing and the old days. That *Newsletter* received a wide local distribution and was a sought after item when it was published each month.

I had been working the waters of Long Island and southern New England for the Lab, with much shipboard time at sea, and had some sea experiences to relate. The baymen, I would learn, were good listeners, too, when it came to sea tales. In the spring of 1974,

Of Baymen and Striped Bass

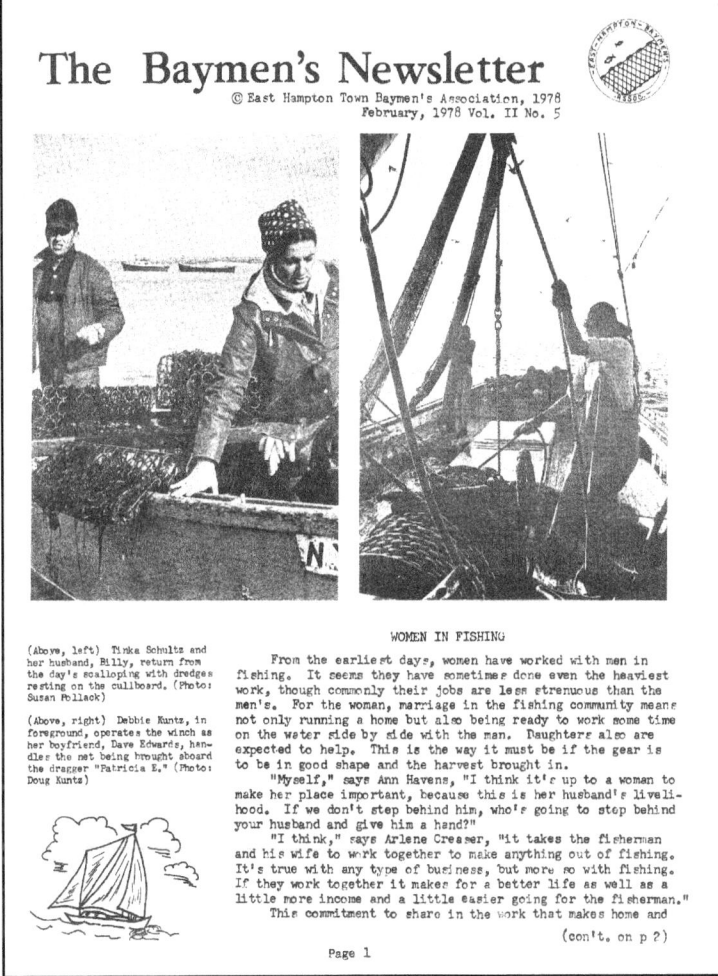

The Baymen's Newsletter. The East Hampton Town Baymen's Association created a Newsletter to communicate with the public. The first issue in June 1974, provided an introduction to the Baymen's Association and its goals. Chief among them were elimination of pollution and preservation of wetlands. I especially liked the Newsletter's interviews with the elder baymen and its articles on the different kinds of traditional fishing methods. The cover of the 1978 issue shown here has a great article on women in fishing. The Newsletter and the enthusiasm that went into it demonstrated the fishing community's interest in reaching out, seeking support from the larger East Hampton community.

On the East End

I represented the Lab and volunteered for a two-week fishery sampling research cruise aboard the NOAA Research Vessel *Albatross IV*, stationed in Woods Hole, Massachusetts. That sampling cruise was 17 days aboard *Albatross IV* in the Northwest Atlantic on Nantucket Shoals, Georges Bank, and Massachusetts Bay for the purpose of sampling the groundfishes on the continental shelf of the mid-Atlantic and New England areas. That experience provided several accounts that the baymen could relate to, since many of them had been to sea for extended periods as crew on offshore draggers or lobster boats. Many of them, now, were independent of those needs to be a crew member and had their own boats and gear, and some had crew members who worked for them for a share of the profits. After we came to know each other better, I occasionally brought my slides and projector to the Association's monthly meetings and presented a short informal show-and-tell of what I was doing at the Lab.

One night, I discussed my two weeks aboard *Albatross IV* and its professional fisherman crew who operated the trawling gear that caught all those "data" for we scientists. That crew really was expert, and they earned their keep best when things went wrong. Broken trawl doors and torn nets 100 miles at sea, during cold rough spring weather, required skill and speed to repair safely. Setting, towing, and retrieving large commercial sized fishing nets at depths of a hundred fathoms in rough spring seas required skill and experience. And a lot of guts! Commercial fishing, I would learn, is an extremely dangerous and hazardous profession, with many injuries and deaths every year at sea. We nearly lost one of the scientists overboard on that cruise due to miscommunications.

When the on-deck scientific sampling work was finished at a sampling station in the Northwest Atlantic, the chief scientist would use the intercom phone to alert the bridge that all was clear, that the work was complete, and that it was OK to begin steaming to the next sampling location. At one sampling location, *Albatross IV* began to steam ahead before the all-clear phone call was made. *Albatross IV*

The NOAA Research Vessel *Albatross IV* berthed in Woods Hole, Massachusetts. The 190-foot long R/V *Albatross IV* was commissioned in the early 1960s as a fully seagoing oceanographic research vessel. I had a memorable two-week adventure aboard *Albatross* in the spring of 1974. There are four levels, or decks, for at-sea work activities. The bottom level is shown in the photo by portholes that are just visible at the level of the dock. This level housed five staterooms each with three bunks and adjoining baths or heads. During rough seas, these portholes would be under water as the vessel rolled in heavy seas. The next level up is shown with a line of ten portholes that housed the galley and mess halls, and the laboratory for processing oceanographic and biological samples. The third level is shown with the line of four portholes. This is the "boat deck" that contained a library and recreation sitting room. The bridge and wheelhouse were on the upper level.

had been running with the seas, in the direction that the ocean waves were moving, while the science crew and fishermen were on the afterdeck securing the equipment for the run to the next sampling location. *Albatross IV* made a turn to starboard and began running broadside to the seas, which made her roll a lot with each wave that met us. On one such roll, a huge wall of green water swept cross the afterdeck and pinned one of the scientists to the port rail, nearly washing her overboard. It was a tense and frightening moment. I was standing in the after-cabin doorway looking out at the deck when

Dangers at Sea. During a spring storm at sea in 1974, the afterdeck of *Albatross IV* was secured for safety. The A-frame and all working booms were lowered and all gear tied down. That storm was so intense that all scientific sampling was curtailed for about 24 hours while we rode out the storm. This photo, taken from the safety of the aftercabin's door, is deceiving. It appears to be looking out onto the level sea. Actually, *Albatross IV* is steaming with the seas and she is in the process of riding up on a wave with her stern facing down into the trough of an oncoming wave behind. Those two weeks aboard *Albatross IV* far out to sea gave me an appreciation for what the Long Island baymen experienced while fishing aboard fishing trawlers and lobster boats out of view of land.

that took place. I was helpless to do anything. Needless to say, communications improved immediately. The baymen understood that account, as they had many such adventures at sea that posed immediate dangers.

Somewhere in the Northwest Atlantic midway in that cruise, *Albatross IV* cut her engines and stopped, as if at some predetermined location. Many of the fishermen and all of the scientific crew assembled on the afterdeck. The ship's master came from the helm carrying an American flag. One of the scientists had a bottle of wine, and another a Bible. A box containing an urn with the ashes of a

Remembering a Friend. A burial at sea aboard the R/V *Albatross IV*, April, 1974. The ship's master, far right, and others hold a flag over an urn containing the ashes of a fellow mariner. The scientist in the yellow oilers read Psalm 107 from the Bible and then a bottle of wine was passed around. The person honored was biologist Robert Hersey.

fellow scientist was placed on a stand and the flag held over it by comrades, one at each corner. The immortal and stirring words of Psalm 107, verses 23–30, were read. It began: *"They that go down to the sea in ships, that do business in great waters; these see the works of the Lord, and his wonders in the deep."* The bottle was opened and passed for all to drink, in a communion-like spirit, under overcast skies, with April winds moving through the rigging and sea birds observing overhead. The urn was removed and the ashes placed overboard at the same geographic location where the departed comrade's father had been returned to sea some years before. The same silence I remember on that afterdeck filled the Marine Museum as the baymen listened. There is a silent unity among seafaring men at the passing of a comrade, even one unnamed and unknown.

Bass on the Backside

I also came to know many of the baymen who fished from the East End's ocean beaches between Amagansett and Montauk, the Backside. Since the main work for East Hampton Town baymen was in the embayments and estuarine waters of the East End, especially those between the North and South Forks of Long Island, on the north side of East Hampton Town, the ocean waters were referred to as the Backside. The ocean fishers used very long nets called haul seines (pronounced haul "sane") that were deployed from ocean dories launched through the surf. At that time, the New York State Department of Environmental Conservation (the DEC) was studying the exploitation and migration of coastal striped bass on Long Island during a three-year study that began in 1973.

The Ocean Science Lab on Montauk provided office and laboratory space to the DEC staff for their East End work, and it was there that I came to know the DEC striped bass research team led by biologist Byron Young. Byron was a likable and jolly guy, about 30 years old, with a permanent grin and infectious laugh, dusty blond hair and a mustache to match. Byron and I had a lot in common and became good friends. He and his fellow DEC fish tagging biologists worked very well together and seemed to enjoy their work thoroughly. They laughed, joked, and needled each other constantly, prompting some of the scientists at the Lab to call them the Department of Environmental "Conversation." Byron knew many of the haul seine fishermen and had a good rapport with most of the fishing crews.

The DEC team had a four-wheel-drive Dodge power wagon that could keep up with the fishermen's trucks on the beach.

DEC Fisheries Crew. The New York State DEC initiated a program of striped-bass research on the East End in 1973. The program began with a biological study of the age, growth, maturity, and migration of striped bass caught by haul seine along the ocean beaches. The original DEC fisheries crew, with whom I worked, are in this photo (left to right) David Obrig, Fred Mushacke, and Byron Young, the crew chief. They are examining the bunt of a haul seine just pulled up onto the beach. They randomly removed legal sized striped bass (those 16" or longer) from the catches, measured and weighed them, removed scales to determine ages, made notes on the general condition and health of the fish, applied a numbered dart tag, and then returned them to the sea.

I accompanied the DEC on many mornings during 1974 and 1975, riding along in their truck. Their cooperation was instrumental in the Lab's being able to gather another two years of data (in addition to the data we gathered during 1972 with Jimmy Lester) on striped bass biology and to publish the findings. We would arrive at the ocean early in the morning and scout the beaches with field glasses looking for a haul seine crew that had found a "set" and was beginning to fish. That done, we drove the beach, met the seiners, and awaited the hauling back of their half mile long seine nets, a process the baymen called "bunting in" or "bunting up." The middle of the long nets had a large and deep pocket called the bunt where the caught fish would be concentrated when the nets were hauled up onto the beach.

The DEC was studying the biology and coastal migrations of New York's legal sized striped bass. New York's minimum length at that time was 16 inches, with no bag limit on how many could be caught by either commercial or recreational fishermen. The other mid-Atlantic coastal states had similar harvest regulations for striped bass. Some had different minimum size limits for legal harvests, but none had bag limits on how many could be caught. Byron had an agreement with the ocean haul seine fishermen to pay them the market price per pound (plus five cents) for all of the striped bass he removed from their catches, tagged and released back to the ocean. The agreement worked, with fishermen and biologists cooperating well, and even helping each other. The DEC crew did not interfere with the fishing operation, but helped empty the net of fish when help was needed. They worked very hard and frantically when removing fish for observation and tagging. They used a large portable container for seawater to hold the bass alive until each could be processed, tagged, and returned to the surf. Byron also kept notes on water temperature, other species taken by the fishermen, and unusual occurrences of fish diseases, injuries, and abnormalities. He documented 75 different species of fishes caught by the haul seiners during that 1973–1975 period, and he wrote about that in his DEC reports. The diversity of fish species in East End marine waters always grabbed our interest.

Our striped bass research at the Lab complimented that of the DEC, since we were interested in studying the short or undersized fish less than 16 inches long. In doing so, we focused mostly on one age group of fish and we studied a segment of the striped bass population often overlooked in fishery research at that time—next year's legal catch. The majority of those short striped bass were two years old and they interested us the most, as they were making their first, of many, annual migrations from their spawning and nursery areas to their northerly summer feeding grounds. By studying one age group of fish (two-year-olds) each year, we were able to monitor successive year classes on their first departure from the home spawning grounds, and thereby observe differences or variations on an annual basis. So, many of those short bass that would have been returned to the sea by the fishermen were returned by us with those numbered red tags. Working with short bass also gave us the advantage of not having to pay for marketable "keepers." The Lab, as a consortium of colleges and universities, was on a lean budget, so the opportunities to accompany the DEC and to obtain fish for study at no cost was an attractive business, as well as a scientific, option. Where we paid, however, was with fish fin spines to the hands, and scales, slime, and sand on all other exposed parts. And with soggy feet, as I wore my low cut at-sea deck boots during this work and not chest waders as did the fishermen and the DEC crew (no budget for waders either).

Those short bass generally weighed between one and two-and-one-half pounds, were glistening silver and white, and were full of spirit. A one-man job to remove scales, weigh, measure, and tag. But try a six-to-ten pound legal sized fish. Two guys to hold it down, maybe. Thrashing, wriggling, squirming, challenging us, daring us to study or understand it. Try your best to treat it gently and return it to the sea unharmed or unstressed. Tag it along the back beneath the dorsal fin with a metal dart insert, like a large hypodermic needle. Carry it 20 yards across the beach to the surf, drop it once, stoop to pick it up while it thrashes sand in your face. Cradle it under one arm, or two, with tail beating for freedom. Finally reach the surf and gently (?) toss it over a breaker. The fish undulates and splashes into the water. Gone! Stand for a moment, watching; be sure he made it and doesn't wash back in. That fish? Go back for another. Oh, ___! Wet feet again. Deck boots! But what an animal, and how I loved working with live fish and lively fishermen.

On the East End

Resource Conflicts

That "ever elusive" spirited coastal traveler, and those stirred human souls, however, lead to conflicts between recreational and commercial fishermen over who caught more fish, over fishing rights, and access to the choice fishing locations along the Atlantic beaches of the East End. The abundant striped bass resource had attracted many participants, many of whom competed for space, as well as for the fish. Each group of fishermen, recreational and commercial, perceived that the bass were being over harvested by the other group. Year after year, the New York State legislature was besieged with proposals to alleviate the problem, legislation generally aimed at constraining the commercial fishing sector. Make the striper a game fish only. Ban gill nets and haul seines. Close Montauk Point to commercial fishing. Ban net fishing off of the state parks. Increase the size limit. And more. I never begrudged the recreational fishery its due, and I certainly enjoyed the sport myself, although I never managed to bring home the really big one. But I was caught up in the conflict, the plight of the traditional fisherman, and what appeared to be a gross misuse of the available scientific data on the species by both fishermen groups and the state legislators. During the winter and spring of 1975, the debate became especially heated, with much press coverage and new legislative proposals. Hot tempers flared between fishing groups. The Baymen's Association shuttled back and forth between Amagansett and Albany talking with legislators. The baymen were at odds with the larger Long Island Fishermen's Association, which considered the conflicts to be an "industry problem" and not just an East End problem. But the East End's haul seine and trap net fisheries were directly affected, so those very independent baymen fought their own battle, or tried to.

I was asked for scientific information and freely gave it, by sharing our research findings that seemed relevant. I talked with aids of State Assembly Speaker Perry Duryea, who lived on Montauk, and showed them the relationships between the abundant Chesapeake Bay production of fish and the harvests in New York, for which there was a direct correlation. I wrote a technical and factual paper to Mr. Duryea and supplied citations to other sources of information, many being studies conducted by the State DEC during the 1960s and early 1970s. There were, I surmised, enough relevant data and studies that, if consulted and used properly, could inject some order, reason, and factual bases into the arguments of who-catches-more-fish, and why the commercial sector shouldn't be more regulated than the recreational sector. There were, at the time, enough fish for all, I thought. Any new conservation management measures should have been applied in some equal way to all of the striped bass resource users, and not to one segment only. New York State, I suggested, could do two important things for striped bass conservation: (1) manage that striped bass habitat over which it had a full measure of control, the Hudson River, versus the Chesapeake Bay where it had no control and where between one-half and two-thirds of the coastal commercial harvest occurred; and (2) work toward the management of striped bass on a multi-state level, since it was an interstate migratory animal.

On April 22, 1975, the Suffolk County Legislature held a one-day hearing in Riverhead, Long Island, on State Assembly Bill No. 3509 that proposed to make striped bass a game fish only. That bill thus proposed to manage the harvest of striped bass in New York State by banning commercial fishing, thinking that recreational fishing only would be sufficient to conserve the fish resource. It was an incorrect assertion. That bill was designed to support the recreational fishermen's belief that commercial fishing was taking too many striped bass, and leaving too few for the recreational harvest. I wrote another factual paper and went to the hearing to testify. I arrived after the hearing room was full and had to stand toward the back in the crowded aisle. I was the last to register to speak, but was called first to testify. I nervously made my way through the crowd to the podium, and opened by stating that I was there to represent a group which had not been heard from yet in any of the legislative proceedings—the striped bass.

That raised some eyebrows and quieted the room. While much of what I said supported the commercial fishermen's stance on the issue, I really tried to be objective and use the best and most relevant scientific information in presenting my suggestions, conclusions, and recommendations. Albert Jensen, a senior biologist with the DEC, also testified that day and independently corroborated much of what I said. Our independent, yet similar, recommendations were helpful, I think, in convincing the legislators that the game fish proposal was of little help in managing striped bass, and that it alone was a poor conservation measure. The entire striped bass resource, and both recreational and commercial fisheries, needed to be managed on an interstate coast-wide basis. Al Jensen offered these and other management measures for New York's striped bass, and other fisheries, in a thoughtful and thought provoking article in the *DEC's New York Fish and Game Journal* in 1977.

A month or so later after that Riverhead hearing, I received in the mail an application form to become a member of the American Institute of Fishery Research Biologists (or AIFRB). It is a professional society of fisheries scientists that elects members upon recommendation and nomination by other members. Its main focus as a society concerns conservation and the maintaining of high professional standards in the practice and application of the science of fishery research biology. One of the criterion for membership includes contributions to the professions and to conservation "in the form of providing expert scientific advice to management councils, international commissions, state management agencies … or promotion of legislation and such other activities concerned with proper management and conservation of fisheries resources." Ethics and professionalism in fisheries research is important to the AIFRB. That was important to me as a field biologist also, so the application for membership was a welcome honor.

I joined the society in 1975 and have been a member ever since. I never did find out who nominated me for membership, but I have long suspected that it was Al Jensen. Al was a senior and well respected fisheries biologist. He had been a researcher and fisheries manager for many years and was a prolific author on fisheries subjects. He wrote a popular book on cod and the codfish fisheries in the northeast, and became known at the "Codfather." Al was a jovial and friendly guy whom I liked and admired. If it was you, Al, thanks. I am privileged to have been an AIFRB member all these years. And I'm pleased to think my efforts, early on in the striped bass management fray, may have helped bring some level of local attention to the needs for equity in management strategies as well as the need for multi-state (or interstate) management of the ever elusive striped bass. In my career as a marine biologist, later turned federal environmental impact assessment professional, striped bass and my work with the Baymen was, and always will be, my professional "numenon" (to use Aldo Leopold's expression). They are an entity without which my career, experience, learning and development would be empty and void.

Science and Society

One of the supporting theories that I offered to the state legislators, however, has since been proven not to be true. I discussed the historical data on striped bass harvests in New York and their relationship to spawning success in Maryland waters of Chesapeake Bay. The two were directly related and there appeared to have been highly successful spawning and survival of striped bass (dominant year classes of fish) at intervals of about six years since the late 1950s. The 1970 year class was the largest and most successful ever recorded for the Chesapeake up to that time, which when coupled with other previous good year classes, had fueled the fishery to record high harvests of striped bass (those 16"-long fish) in 1973. If the six-year pattern continued, I theorized, then 1976 would be another good year class, followed by continued good fishing. 1976 was, in fact, a less-than-average year class, and was followed by several poor year classes. The Chesapeake stock was indeed in a period of decline, as were the spawning stocks in other states. The boom days of striped bass fishing were about to approach a bust.

The health of the Chesapeake Bay declined, along with many of its traditional fin- and shellfisheries. The Hudson River striped bass fishery was closed due to PCB contamination, and the entire New York coastal market was affected. The coastal striped bass fishery was on its way to being economically depleted. The striped bass fisheries along the mid-Atlantic Coast were closed entirely in 1985 in an interstate effort to manage the resource and aid its recovery. Traditional fisheries and people's leisure were reduced to spectator sports. It was suggested to me by a colleague that striped bass management was in such disarray, then, and the New York fisheries so threatened, that in order to cope, the East End baymen would have to stop being "Bonackers," and being so independent, stubborn, and old fashioned in accepting management initiatives designed to protect the fish stocks.

While there may have been some truth to that, asking the baymen not to be themselves would be like asking an eagle to stop soaring on thermals between mountain peaks. Or like asking a striped bass not to ride the tidal currents or chase baitfish into the surf. Like asking a seafaring man to sit on the shore and watch. The coastal striped bass resource depletion was reversed by that fishery closure and by a series of coast-wide conservation measures that restricted the harvests in terms of bag limits, greatly increased legal minimum size limits for harvest (as great as 38" for a brief time, then lowered to a coast-wide 28"), seasonal fishing closures and area closures during critical spawning times, and other measures to control the harvest and sale

Of Baymen and Striped Bass

Striped-Bass Fishing in the Past. The author, at right, with friend Terry O'Riordan, after an early morning of striped-bass fishing in Fort Pond Bay, Montauk, in the spring of 1973. That morning netted 30 keeper bass all in excess of the 16-inch minimum legal length for bass at that time. There was no bag limit on how many legal-sized bass could be kept. We were careful to return alive and unharmed the undersized short bass we caught. We stocked our freezers with those fish that fall and gave away some to family and friends. There was no waste of those we kept.

of fish. Managing the striped as an interstate migratory animal succeeded and the management program has since served as a model for other fisheries in need of conservation.

So many people seeking such a desirable sport and food fish, along with changing or deteriorating environmental conditions in the species' East Coast natal waters, have rendered the halcyon or hey-days of relatively unrestricted fishing for striped bass as a thing of the past. Also in the past is commercial haul seine fishing for striped bass on the East End's ocean beaches, which was banned permanently by the State of New York in 1990. While ocean beach haul seine fishing for other species was permitted, striped bass was the "money fish," rendering that method of harvest as a potentially profitable one. When striped bass no longer could be harvested by haul seine, the entire operation became economically questionable, thus a local traditional means of working, living, and harvesting fish was made a historical thing of the past. The baymen also have been affected by deteriorating environmental conditions in the East End bays that have reduced or eliminated fishing for other important species like bay scallops and hard clams. Offshore fish stocks for several species have declined making their pursuit more costly with less return. The burgeoning local population, with resulting tremendous changes to the landscape, water quality, a reduction in open space, and a significant increase in the cost of living all have compounded the local baymen's community. The era of the true opportunistic all-season bayman who follows the weather, tides, seasons, fishes, and shellfishes also may be approaching a historical thing of the past. It saddens me to think, feel, or to write this.

I look back on my time on the East End and the baymen with much satisfaction and even nostalgia. Time does that. But I also recall my involvement with the striped bass fishery and the legislative issues into which I tried to inject some reason and science. My error, my *mea culpa*, in theorizing and qualitatively forecasting incorrectly the future abundance of the striped bass resource still haunts me. That involvement was where science and the humanities intersect. Science can help society describe and understand the workings of nature and the environment, and understand what may need to be done to correct human induced environmental problems or to manage environmental change.

Science alone, however, cannot make the changes happen. That must come from the humanities and the social systems that work within society and govern its workings and the behavior of people pursuing fish. Elected officials, legislators, lawyers, public communicators, and news reporters must use the scientific information in ways that work for society. And the citizenry must be willing to abide by the societal decisions based on the science. Garrett Hardin termed this creation of environmental regulations as "mutual coercion, mutually agreed upon." Sometimes society chooses to do other than the science recommends.

My attempt to forecast the future of striped bass fishing in New York State didn't help manage the resource or alleviate the resource management issue. Part of the problem was that the conservation and biological studies on New York's striped bass fisheries were underway and incomplete at that time. I had used current, yet incomplete, information. My involvement at least put some scientific information into the public debate and, I hope, got the message to the legislators that only conservation of the entire fishery resource on an interstate level was likely to have any success. The Atlantic coast-wide scientific study of the striped bass resource and the eventual closure of the fisheries in subsequent years did combine with the social systems to bring order and renewed conservation management, even at the expense of some segments of the traditional fishery. Today, striped bass abound on the East Coast, an outcome that makes me smile.

Scientists don't like to err in their areas of specialization, however, and many avoid interaction with the public process and the press for fear of being used, abused, and misquoted. I've been there. But I did the best I could with the information at hand, and tried to help. What I also recall is that help, to my psyche at least, was returned several fold. Newspaper accounts then reported kindly of my involvement and my factual information. Many baymen I hardly knew went out of their way to speak to me or just say hi after that. When I was introduced to Scotty Eames, an elderly and respected bayman, he was asked "Do you know Corky?" (my nickname). He answered, "Sure, everyone knows Corky." It took me some time to really appreciate his comment.

One morning in the spring of 1975 following that legislative hearing in Riverhead, I was on the beach with Byron Young preparing to process and tag striped bass with the haul seiners, when we approached a haul seine crew loading their net back into the ocean dory. The dory sat up high on a trailer being towed by a bright red Dodge power wagon. It was the Havens family crew, with several relatives and several generations. The crew leader, William Havens ("Mr." Havens to most everyone) was a sixth generation descendant of local fishermen and whalers. He was a public spirited man, a WWII veteran, and a founding member of the Town Baymen's Association. We sought the Havens crew often. They were knowledgeable and able fishermen who often caught fish. They didn't waste a set and a whole morning's work hunting blindly. They were smart fishermen, and rugged, every one of them. We drove near, stopped the truck, and walked up to the dory. Billy Havens, one of Mr. Havens' sons, was hard at work hauling the big seine back into the dory and stacking it properly for the next set. As we approached, he stopped, leaned on the rail, and waved down to me. "Hi, Corky!" he said with a big smile. With a meager crackling voice, all I could get out was "Hi, Billy …."

Ocean Haul Seining

It was a thrilling sight to watch the haul seine operation and see a pickup truck launch a dory into the ocean surf. I've personally been in the surf, lots of times. I surfed the Jersey shores in the 1960s and even tried once at Ditch Plain on Montauk in the mid-1970s. The ocean and I have a long-standing relationship. But to see a truck up to its running boards in salt water and sand was very exciting, and a bit disturbing. The fishing operation began in the early morning hours when the shadows on the beach were very long and pointed westerly. Two pickup trucks would make their way along the beach. Both had their standard metal beds removed and replaced with much wider and deeper wooden beds with wooden rails around. The capstan head of a power winch sat in the front of the bed near the cab. There are five or six fishermen. One was elderly, two or three middle-aged, and the rest younger in their 20s or 30s. One truck pulled a long, large ocean dory on a specially made trailer. The dory-truck made a low and powerful roar as it moved slowly along the beach, riding in the deep tracks of soft sand made earlier by another such vehicle. In fact, once the truck was is in those deep sandy tracks, the driver took his hands off the wheel. It went just fine, and did in fact, seem to take on a life, an animation, of its own. I recall the Havens' bright red trucks, sitting high on heavy-duty suspension, with oversized tires. They had a low mellow roar and crept along, with steering wheels moving in response to the front wheels feeling their way along an existing trail on the beach, almost like being on auto-pilot. Almost like a bloodhound on a taut leash sniffing the trail and leading the way to the quarry.

A bayman pointed seaward. Out beyond the surf the glassy complexion of the ocean was disturbed and active. Gulls and terns began to arrive and worked the surface for a fish meal. A school of small baitfish, probably silversides, anchovy, or sand lance, was being chased by larger predators, perhaps striped bass or bluefish. The word was given by Mr. Havens, the haul seine crew leader, and the big truck towing the dory came to life with a roar and turned toward the dunes. Once aligned perpendicular to the ocean, it backed down the berm of the beach until the trailer was very near the water on hard wet sand. It stopped. The crew became excited, nervous, serious. Two fishermen, one middle aged, the other younger, climbed into the dory. An outboard motor was mounted on an engine well toward one end of the boat. The motor, raised up and out of the well, was lowered and tested.

It worked. The surf was rolling in and the truck driver awaited a lull, a "slatch," between breakers. The outboard was restarted. The lull came. The truck groaned and backed the trailer quickly into the slatch between breakers, and then stopped abruptly. In one motion, the purring outboard was tipped into the engine well as the dory slid off the trailer and into the water. It moved seaward through the

Preparing to Set. The Havens family fishing crew readying their ocean dory and haul seine net for launching into the surf on a calm May morning in 1974. The haul seine fishermen worked primarily during spring and fall when the desirable fishes were migrating along the coast. Striped bass was a sought after species that always had market. It could be sold to local markets and restaurants or shipped into New York City. Other good eating food fishes like bluefish sometimes would be caught in abundance but returned to the sea when there was a glut of them on the market. When there was a harvest, the day's take from the sale was divided among the crew members, one share to each fishermen, and one share each to the owner of the trucks and the dory.

breakers and began paying out the long seine net over the rail. There were markers along the float line of the net at length intervals that alerted the fishermen as to how much net was released and when to turn the dory. At the mid-point, the net's bunt was pushed overboard. At another marker point, the dory was turned shoreward and run back up to the beach. The truck with the trailer met the dory in the surf and used a line tethered to the boat, and wrapped around the power winch, to pull it back onto the trailer. The two trucks then were positioned at each end of the long net and were several hundred yards apart on the beach. Each truck had a long rope line to one

Completing the Set. The Havens family ocean haul seine crew in the process of retrieving their dory from the surf. After setting or laying the long haul seine in a semicircle pattern out from the ocean beach, the empty dory is met by a truck and trailer. The dory is driven up onto the submerged trailer and secured, and the truck then pulls it out of the surf and up onto the beach. This truck is tethered by a line to a second truck on higher ground in case it gets stuck in the wet sand and surf. It could be especially hazardous launching and retrieving a haul-seine dory on days of high or heavy surf and required skill and experience. There are many local stories of surfmen drowned and injured in this dangerous profession.

end of the haul seine. When the crew chief gave the order, the winchmen standing in the beds of the trucks wrapped the long lines around the winch capstan heads and began using the power takeoffs to haul the seine ashore. Years ago, this hauling was done by hand, before such powerful trucks were available. Once the bunt was out of the surf and up on the beach, the fishermen sorted the fish for keepers and returned the rest to the ocean.

That scene always brought to mind the accounts I have read of the townsfolk of a century ago flocking to the beaches in response to a bell-call that a shoal (school) of fish, or a whale, was near shore.

On the East End

Securing the Dory. The Havens family fishing crew securing their dory onto its trailer after setting their ocean haul seine from the beach at Amagansett on an early May morning in 1974. Fishing always began early in the morning, as indicated here by the long shadows pointing westward. My shadow is to the right as I photographed this scene. The self reliance and independence of those baymen appealed to me, as did the early morning fisheries work on quiet and beautiful beaches of the East End. By the time I was doing that work in the mid-1970s, I already was an accomplished and indigenous member of the beach fauna from my earlier years in the 1960s on the New Jersey shore. "Beach Bum" is one of my core competencies.

Dories would be rolled across the beach on log rollers and rowed through the surf in hot pursuit. Technology has improved upon those techniques, but the thrill and nervous energy were the same. At least mine was. Those early spring mornings on the beaches, working with live fish and lively people, were among the most fun, delightful, and rewarding on-the-job experiences I have ever had. The lessons I learned there about fish, fisheries, fishermen, science and society have stayed with me and influenced me ever since.

Steeped in History. Bow of the Havens's ocean dory, looking particularly shark-like. A truck is pulling it slowly along the beach at the end of the fishing operation. The large seine net is being stacked back into the dory and made ready for another set. I recall that the dory used by bayman Danny King's crew was painted as an American flag, prompting some to refer to it as the "American Dory." Commercial fishing in the ocean off of the East End's beaches traces its roots back to the 1800s when whaling boats and cod-fishing dories were rolled down the beach on wooden logs and then rowed through the surf. The nets then were retrieved by a crew of men hauling the seines onto the beaches by hand.

Respect and Generosity

Those East End people were among the most giving and generous people I've known. When there were storms and power outages, or a death in the family, the locals took care of each other, offering food and shelter to those in need. I recall with much admiration how the baymen respected their elders. Aging baymen no longer able to captain a fishing boat or handle an ocean dory through the surf would take on less strenuous, yet still important, fishing crew positions. Jimmy Lester's grandfather, William J. Lester, "Cap'n Bill," was an admired and respected bayman who fished well into his 80s. His fishing roots went back several generations to Lesters who hunted whales off the East End beaches before the American Civil War. Fishing was not a job or a career for such a traditional bayman, it was his life. I saw Cap'n Bill working with an ocean haul seine crew, in the 1970s. He fished with Dominic Grace's crew for a while then. I believe that he was the winchman in the truck, hauling back the morning's catch. Bill was respected for his years on the water and his knowledge and wisdom of fishing. There is a great lesson there, one that our youth-focused modern society is loosing.

I recall also one morning fishing with the Havens family haul seine crew. The seine was being hauled back onto the beach by two trucks and their winchmen. The bunt was bulging with fish and about to burst. It was so big and heavy-laden with fish that the power winches could not pull it up the steep beach face and out of the surf. The power takeoff in one of the trucks groaned and slowed down under the heavy load and was about to stall out. A stall of the engine and power winch would have let the bunt and the net slide back into the surf where it would have been pummeled and ripped apart, possibly destroying the net and releasing its valuable contents. As this scene unfolded, another haul seine crew was driving up the beach from the east en route home after completing their fishing. It was the Lester family crew.

One of the fishermen, a younger son of Cap'n, Bill named Calvin Lester, saw the Havens' predicament and reacted instinctively. He jumped out of his truck and into the cab of the Havens' truck that was groaning and about to stall. He stepped on the accelerator and gave the power takeoff a burst of new energy. With his foot on the accelerator, he watched through the cab's rear window view of the beach and fishing operation and adjusted the winch speed to just what was needed to haul the bulging net ashore. I think that Calvin may have saved the Havens' entire morning of fishing and their unusually large harvest that day. Those ocean haul seine fishing crews were very competitive in those times, vying for the best fishing spots on the beach and for getting to market first each day with their harvests to maximize profits. They even competed for the best fishermen to be members of their crews. But when help was needed in a tight spot, those local people stood together.

I will never forget watching the intensity on Calvin's face as he struggled to help his friends, even though they were

•

the competition. Peter Matthiessen in his classic book on East End commercial fishing, *Men's Lives*, describes an incident in 1974 in which Calvin came to the aid of Jens Lester's ocean haul seine crew. Jens' steel dory was swamped in heavy seas and sank while being launched into the ocean surf. Calvin helped rescue the fishermen. In the years since then, many baymen have stopped their all-season traditional ways of fishing, for several reasons. But I have heard that Calvin still fishes "in the old way." Guess he learned well from Cap'n Bill.

The East End's Influence

Those people of the East End, their teachings, and my time in that marine coastal environment have remained with me in spirit ever since I left the East End in 1975. In early 1976, I took a staff position as a fishery biologist with the U.S. Nuclear Regulatory Commission at its Washington, DC, headquarters. I got a tip on that job opening from Dr. J. Laurence McHugh, professor of fisheries at Stony Brook. One of Professor McHugh's former students had held the position that was vacated at the NRC, a position I stepped into in early 1976. At that time, there were many nuclear-fueled electric generating stations, power plants, under construction across the country.

The NRC was the federal agency charged with the responsibility to license both the construction and the eventual operation of those power plants. The licensing process included an evaluation by the NRC of the environmental impacts of constructing and operating those large industrial facilities. Power plants all use large volumes of water to cool the electric generators that produce the electricity, thus they are sited on large bodies of water, such as the ocean, bays, estuaries, lakes, or rivers. Some even have constructed their own artificial cooling lakes as part of the power plant industrial site. The large volumes of cooling water needed for the power plants meant that once the plants began operating, they had the potential to adversely affect the aquatic environment, including the fisheries. Even during the construction of the plants, there was the potential for industrial construction activities to affect the aquatic environment. I spent nearly 12 years on the NRC staff working on those aquatic environmental matters.

One such case I was assigned to by the NRC, and an adventure that stands high in my career and life experience, involved the commercial fishing community of Seabrook, New Hampshire, during the fall of 1977. The Seabrook Nuclear Plant was under construction at a site on the landward side of a large estuary and salt marsh on the New Hampshire coast. New Hampshire has a fourteen-mile coastline on the Gulf of Maine, with the Hampton–Seabrook Estuary a prominent feature. That estuary is shaped very much like Accabonac Creek in East Hampton Town, with long channels and arms running north and south from a central harbor entrance. The Hampton–Seabrook Estuary, however, is many times larger than Accabonac Creek and can accommodate large boats. The Town of Seabrook, along with Seabrook Harbor, is located near the estuary's entrance and on its south end.

The town of Seabrook is home to a commercial fishing and lobstering community that reminded me very much of Long Island's East End and its baymen. During the latter part of October and early November of 1977, there was a mass mortality (a kill) of lobsters being held alive by the lobstermen in pounds and wooden pens that were anchored and floating in Seabrook Harbor. As many as 3400 lobsters worth up to about $10,000 to the lobsterman had died. The local press picked up on the event and ran several stories. Some press accounts suggested that the Seabrook Nuclear Plant's nearby construction activities were responsible for the lobster deaths. The Plant's main construction site was about a half mile or so from the Harbor area, but a barge unloading site for the Plant was being constructed very near the location in the harbor where the dead lobsters had been housed. Part of the barge site construction involved pumping water out of the construction area as it was being back filled with sand. It was thought that this dewatering effluent might have created a siltation problem that killed the lobsters.

Since the press accounts and some of the local public were concerned that construction activities of the Seabrook Nuclear Plant might be responsible for the lobster deaths, the NRC decided to investigate the incident. Since I was a marine biologist with northeast commercial fisheries experience, I was assigned to look into the matter. I made several phone calls to the utility company that was constructing the Plant, as well as to the New Hampshire Fish and Game Department, and to several other state and federal agencies with some interest in the matter. After gathering enough preliminary information, I went to the site in New Hampshire to see for myself just what had happened. I asked one of the biologists with the Fish and Game Department, Mr. Edward (Ted) Spurr, if he could arrange for me to meet with some of the lobstermen who had lost lobsters during the mortality event.

Ted was a very nice and amicable guy who spoke in a low slow voice with a New England accent. He said that he wasn't sure that it would be possible, but he would try. I went to Seabrook on December 1, 1977. I was not long away from the East End then, either, as I had been with the NRC for less than two years. My position with NRC was a fishery biologist and I felt like I still had some salt water in my veins (left over from several years of field marine fisheries work in New York), even though my NRC work was mostly in an office in Bethesda, Maryland. December 1st was a gray overcast and damp day. I wore a warm Navy pea coat with a high collar, my Greek fisherman's hat, and my old 1966 Army boots. I spent the afternoon observing the Plant construction site and the barge site near where the lobsters had died.

That evening after dark, I went with Ted Spurr to the small fishing village of Seabrook at the head of Seabrook Harbor. We drove through the village and up to a small house and stopped. We then walked around the house to what looked like a garage or working outbuilding behind. I was a bit nervous, but it began to feel familiar there. Many of the baymen from the East End whom I had known and worked with in Amagansett and East Hampton also had similar backyard working buildings. Bayman Jimmy Lester spent much of his non-fishing time in his outbuilding working on his fishing gear. He also built a small boat there and overhauled his dragger there.

As Ted and I approached the outbuilding, I noticed that it was well lit inside. I peered through a window as we walked around to the door. I saw a local policeman in uniform standing along the wall, and about a dozen other men standing around the periphery of the room inside. "Oh, boy," I thought, "do we need a policeman for this tonight?" My nervousness heightened. I sensed that Ted, too, was a bit uneasy. We went inside and Ted exchanged some pleasantries with some of the men. They were all local lobstermen and commercial fishermen. The police officer was a relative of some of the lobstermen, and just there to observe. Ted introduced me and talked briefly about my being from Washington and wanting to figure out just what had happened with the lobster kills.

I stood more or less in the middle of the room, and used a crate as a place to set my notebook while we talked. I explained that I was a marine biologist and that I had known and worked with the East Hampton Town Baymen's Association on Long Island. The NRC, therefore, had asked me to look into the lobster deaths in relation to the Seabrook Nuclear Plant's construction activities. I explained what I was trying to do and that I needed their help, if they would be willing to share their knowledge and information with me. I recall having an interesting couple of hours or so of conversation and information gathering. I asked if any of the lobstermen present would give me their names and the amount of lobsters they had lost. Seven men did.

Of Baymen and Striped Bass

I was a bit surprised, yet pleased, at their cooperation with me, a stranger and a fed from Washington. I think that being on their turf (literally), being with Ted, asking for their assistance (but not trying to force it), and being dressed in my usual pea coat greatly facilitated the evening. Also, I respected them and their profession, as I had learned from the baymen. Actually, being in that garage with those men that night brought back many good and nostalgic feelings of being a member of the Baymen's Association and the monthly evening meetings that were held in the basement of the Marine Museum on Bluff Road in Amagansett. I loved those meetings and I loved the fact that I, a scientist from the Montauk Lab, was accepted by the Baymen as a member. I took good notes at Seabrook that evening and got a lot of useful information for my investigation, from the people directly affected in the matter. I had been a good listener.

At the end of our conversation in the garage, I asked a few of the lobsterman if I could see a lobster car and a lobster pound, the kind in which the lobsters had died. They were eager to show me, so off we walked to a beach at the head of Seabrook Harbor where there was a wooden lobster car on shore. One of the lobsterman explained what it was and how it worked. Essentially, it was a floating pen made of heavy wood, and measuring about 10' long by 8' wide and 4'–5' deep. It was divided into four equal sized compartments for holding lobsters until they could be taken to market. I recall all of us standing around the lobster car in the dark, with some headlights shining on it, talking about it as I looked inside, poked it, felt it and generally got a good mental picture of just what it was like.

Afterwards, we walked into another building nearby to see an indoor lobster pound owned by one of the men. It was a series of shallow wooden tanks or troughs, holding live lobsters, with continuously circulating seawater pumped from the harbor. We discussed it at some length. We also talked about the lobster industry, their fishing, and how they handled their catches. It was a very good evening, one I enjoyed immensely. It felt familiar and made me miss the East

End, something I have done ever since leaving in 1975. I think that Ted was a bit surprised at what had happened and how much cooperation was shown by the lobstermen that evening. I sensed that there may have been some difficulties between the local commercial fishermen and the New Hampshire Fish and Game Department, even though Ted seemed to be in tune with them. I had seen the same thing on Long Island between the commercial fishermen and the New York State Department of Environmental Conservation, the state's fishery regulatory agency, even though some of the DEC biologists seemed to be in tune with the needs of the fishing industry.

I returned to my office in Bethesda, Maryland, and continued to work on the investigation. In February 1978, the *National Fisherman*, a commercial fishing industry trade publication, ran a story on the lobster kills and cited me as the NRC investigator. I had received a phone call from one of the publication's reporters regarding the investigation and the results, which I freely shared. It was not unusual for me to be named in media accounts of NRC cases on which I worked. Most of my cases either resulted in a written public report or impact assessment of some type that were made public as a result of public hearings or meetings. NRC issued an official public technical report in 1978, which I authored, on the lobster kill incident. It described and analyzed the Seabrook lobster kill matter and concluded that several factors in combination were involved in creating the mass mortality. A combination of unusual and stressful natural environmental circumstances plus the presence of an extremely virulent bacterial lobster disease, called gaffkemia or red-tail disease, appeared to have been responsible. Many of the lobsters had been crowded into the holding cars, a condition that is conducive to the spread of the disease. I sent copies of the final report to all the lobstermen who had assisted my investigation and to the various state and federal agencies involved.

I believe that one of the reasons I was able to bring the Seabrook lobster kill matter to closure was that I was willing to interact personally with the "affected public." I tried not to be that arrogant and bureaucratic "holier-than-thou" drone from Washington when I met with the fishermen in Seabrook. I did not fake the mariner look; I really liked my pea coat and wore it all the time to my federal job in Bethesda. It made me feel a bit nautical at a time in my life when I was very much missing my seacoast roots and connectedness with the sea. My local New Hampshire colleague, Ted Spurr, was of much assistance in that matter. I admired Ted and was a bit envious of him. Whenever I was assigned to an environmental case by the NRC, I sought out local experts, like Ted, for information and assistance. They were invaluable and I wanted to be one of them, again. I actually was becoming such a local expert in fishes and fisheries when I lived and worked on the East End. When I left there I lost that and a bit of who I was.

Of Brookers and Bonackers

Some years after that Seabrook experience, my daughter's high school in Maryland participated in a band exchange with a high school in Hampton, New Hampshire. Her band went to New Hampshire, played a concert in Hampton, and then the students had some cultural time in Hampton Beach and in Boston. The New Hampshire school then came to Maryland for a similar experience. Three girls in the band stayed with us and we had some lengthy conversations about New Hampshire and Seabrook. The girls called the Seabrook citizens "Brookers," a term I had not heard during my travels there. I wasn't sure if the term was an affectionate one or not. The Brookers I met, however, reminded me very much of the Bonackers I knew on Long Island's East End.

The Brookers were commercial fishermen named Littlefield (several individuals), Brown, Randall, Fowler, and Butler. The commercial fishing Bonackers I knew and worked with were from families named Lester (several families and several generations), Havens, King, Edwards, Vorpahl, Bennett, Wood, and several others. Those Brookers in New Hampshire and the Bonackers on Long Island all were fishermen by background and upbringing, it seemed. Fishing was not just a job or a career from which they ultimately would retire. They were gatherers and harvesters of the sea. They lived and worked with the seasons, the tides, and the weather. Fishing and the sea was their life, their very being, it was who they were. The real true East End bayman is a "fisher-of-all-trades" who changes his pursuit and his gear with the seasons and the whims of those resources he pursues. I learned about commercial fishing as *life and being* from those Bonackers on the East End and from the Baymen's Association. Those people and those lessons now are part of my being and my upbringing.

Rebuilding Fish Stocks and a Human Community

I am greatly disturbed to learn now that many East End baymen have fallen on hard fishing and economic times. The changing quality and environmental degradation of the once pristine East End estuaries and marine waters may be contributing to altered finfish and shellfish populations, and thus to reduced harvests. Even those baymen who traditionally have changed from one species fishery to another are having a hard time, as the diversity of fishery types has diminished, or as some coastal management measures have restricted harvests. Some baymen tell their sons now not to be a fisherman, as they are, but to get another more reliable and better paying job, a job on the land.

I fear that pretty soon there may not be any more elderly and respected Cap'n Bills left. Sons and daughters won't work beside and learn from their baymen fathers and grandfathers any more. A traditional American way of life then will be as endangered as some of those revered species we work so hard to restore and protect. These individual fishermen are small businessmen in an era when small no longer is competitive. Small farms give way to larger ones. "Mom and Pop" stores are put out of business by the larger chain firms. Are the baymen to go the same way?

After the East Coast striped bass stock plummeted along the entire mid-Atlantic region in the late 1970s and mid-1980s, haul seining for striped bass was stopped by the State of New York in 1990. It has not been allowed to resume, even though coast-wide conservation measures have been especially successful in revitalizing the striped bass resource. When such traditional ways of fishing, and thus traditional livelihoods, become endangered, so too does the very identity of the fishers and indeed the whole community in which they live and work. Haul seining seems as a "numenon" of the East End, an entity without which the entire landscape seems void and incomplete. It would seem reasonable to expect that a revitalized and viable striped bass resource that is fished by many commercial and recreational means could accommodate a limited haul seine fishery. One goal for attaining a sustainable environment should include supporting traditional cultures, and in this case traditional fisheries. Fishery management programs need to incorporate human needs, work within established local values, and help to build community as much as possible while regulating human behavior in relation to the environment. It seems a bit unfair that the haul seine fishermen who assisted the DEC in the striped bass conservation studies have not been able to share in the reward of a striped bass harvest. The State DEC did offer a very small and tightly regulated harvest of striped bass by haul seine in the mid-1990s. That potential harvest apparently was not considered to be economically viable by the baymen and it never was pursued.

The process of hauling the large seine net out of the surf and dragging it up onto the beach face sometimes can inflict a high mortality to undersized striped bass, and to captured fishes of all species, especially when the bunt is full and bulging. Overcoming this, may be but an issue of creating a new or innovative net design, or haul seine fishing technique, that would result in a greater survival of captured fishes that could be returned to the sea alive. Perhaps such an innovative design, that is more resource friendly, could include a way to empty the net while it still is in the water. A joint design effort by the State DEC and the baymen might pay off for both. A revived haul seine fishery also may need the fishermen to exercise their special form of ethical fishing behavior in trying to return to the sea alive as many captured fishes as possible that are not marketable. A return of some form of legal haul seining for striped bass would revive the tradition of ocean fishing from the beaches, a tradition going back to the whalers and cod fishermen. With new nets and procedures, and a reduced mortality of captured fishes returned to the sea, perhaps a renewed effort of monitored and regulated fishing by haul seine would help the East End to affirm its history and identity and to regain a piece of itself.

The degrading environmental conditions of the East End's marine environment and the deterioration of the fisheries are not just the fisherman's or the fishing families' dilemma. They are a dilemma for all of society. As eastern Long Island has become more populace and the East End has grown, one consequence of a burgeoning people is change to the landscape, along with related changes to the environmental quality of the watershed and estuarine and marine waters into which the watershed flows. These are societal issues and consequences that need to be addressed by **all** who have an interest in and a stake in the natural environmental quality of the East End. East End "stakeholders" are everyone, all of us, all the permanent residents of the East End, those with second homes and vacation homes, all of the tourists who visit seasonally, all of the sport fishing people who come from nearby counties, and several states around, to partake of the East End's natural bounty, and all who do business there regardless of where their place of business is housed. The changing nature of the traditional baymen is but one symptom of much larger societal actions and society-induced environmental perturbations. It is an environmental indicator of sorts, a canary in the East End environmental and sociological mine. It will take **all** of we stakeholders aligned together to work on this problem of our East End environmental commons.

3

Fishing with Jimmy

"H'lo, Bub," Jimmy said, as I approached.

"H'lo, Cap," I answered.

"Ready t' go?"

"Yup."

"You're it today. My regular crewman Joe's got another job this mornin.'"

"Then you're in trouble, with a scien'ist for a crew."

"Sometimes you're good luck, if the boat don't sink." I'd heard that one before.

"I do remember a fall day a few years back when you took a big bunch of striped bass, because *I* was there. **Somebody's** gotta help you catch fish," I replied

"Wearin' those cheap lab boots? Hope you didn't bring that damn clipboard! Let's go."

It was 5:30 AM during the spring in the mid-1980s. My family was visiting old friends in Amagansett on one of our visits to the East End. I walked to bayman Jimmy Lester's home on Montauk Highway from our friend's place off Schellinger Road. Jimmy and I climbed into his pickup and drove east toward Montauk. The drive from Amagansett took us along Montauk Highway and down onto the several mile long sandy isthmus that connects the Village of Amagansett with the Village of Montauk to the east. Montauk is as far east as you can go in New York State. There used to be a sign along the roadway pointing easterly and saying "Montauk, Last Stop Before Portugal."

The sandy isthmus runs easterly from Amagansett, with the Atlantic Ocean beach at Napeague to the south and the estuary of Napeague Harbor to the north. Locally, the isthmus is called the "Napeague stretch." In geological terms, it actually is a tombolo, a low lying sandy spit between two landmasses or islands. The Napeague stretch tombolo was formed when the last glaciers receded about 12,000 years ago. Weathering of the land masses at either end, and the action of the ocean currents and surf, washed and shaped the sand form in between what was the mainland at Amagansett and the land that may have been two islands now forming Hither Hills and Montauk.

During the 1800s, the farmers from East Hampton and Amagansett would drive their cattle along the Napeague stretch onto Montauk's grasslands for summer grazing. Entering Montauk felt very much like arriving at an island, thus the cattle were driven "on," or "onto," Montauk and not "to" Montauk. They then went "off" Montauk as

Fishing with Jimmy

View of Montauk in the 1970s. An aerial view looking southeasterly across the center of the Montauk peninsula circa 1971–1972. The Atlantic Ocean is seen running across the entire top of this view. The body of water to the upper left is a portion of Lake Montauk, where the harbor is located (but out of this view). The body of water to the right center is Fort Pond, a fresh-water lake running north to south. At one time, Fort Pond had a narrow neck of water reaching northerly almost to Fort Pond Bay, which is shown running along the entire bottom of this view. That narrow neck of water sometimes opened to the Bay during spring allowing the influx of both salt water and migrating alewives. Just prior to 1900, the railroad came onto Montauk and its tracks permanently blocked any connection between Fort Pond and the Bay.

well. Those expressions still held in the 1970s, for people visiting Montauk, especially among the local people. Those expressions and feelings appear to be changing today, however, as "going to" Montauk seems more common, as does referring to what's happening "in Montauk" village.

That morning in the mid-1980s was fair and sunny, with only a light wind blowing. We drove along the Napeague stretch, onto Montauk, and went straight to Montauk Harbor through Hither

Hills on the main highway. In Montauk Village, we turned north on Edgemere Road and drove past the old New York Ocean Science Laboratory site. It was right next to the Montauk Railroad Station, the end of the line for the Long Island Railroad. I could not help looking at it as we passed by. I strained to see as much of the site as I could, wondering what was going on there, if anything. The grass was cut. No cars in the parking areas. No flag flying. Empty and kind of spooky. The Lab had closed in 1982 due to financial problems. I turned and looked forward. Jimmy glanced at me. Nothing was said.

On Days of No Weather

On fair mornings when Jimmy was sure he "had weather" good enough for tending and lifting his pound net fish traps, we went straight to the Harbor to board his work boat. On mornings when the wind was blowing hard and Jimmy had doubts about being able to get to his fish traps and tend them, we would go to Gosman's Dock, at the west jetty of the Montauk Harbor entrance on Block Island Sound, to check on the sea conditions. If we didn't have favorable weather and couldn't get to the traps in Fort Pond Bay in Jimmy's dragger, I would be a little disappointed at no opportunity to renew my acquaintance with the sea and its bounty. A deck load of fish and squid was an anticipated event, one I waited all year for. Many a cold winter since I left the Lab in 1975 had been spent reading the fishing report and naturalist Larry Penny's "Nature Notes" in the *East Hampton Star* or reading some books on local East End history obtained during those annual visits. I still had the East End and the sea in my blood.

Even with no weather, Jimmy did not (and probably could not) go right home. We would sit at the jetty for a spell and watch the fishing fleet emigrate from the Harbor: trawlers of all sizes and varieties, lobster boats, and sport-fishers. Jimmy knew many of the captains and fishermen, and answered my questions about the vessels and

Fishing with Jimmy

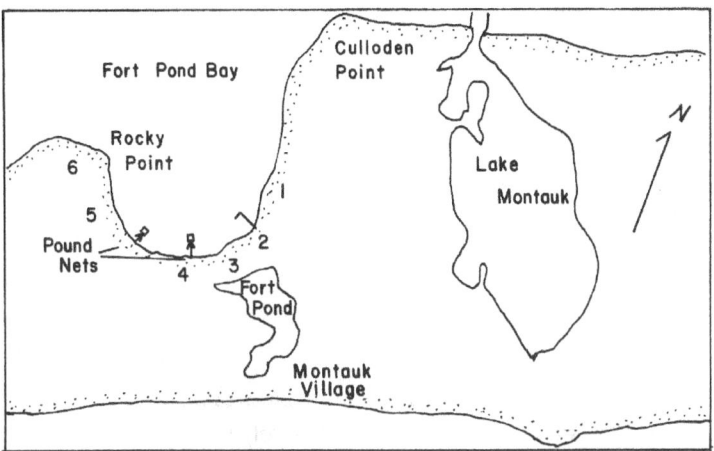

Fort Pond Bay, Montauk. Map of Fort Pond Bay on Montauk, and the location of Bayman Jimmy Lester's two pound traps on the Bay's southern shore. Montauk is about 20 miles from the coast of New England and about 130 miles from Manhattan.

their quarry. Other fishermen would come and go by pickup at the jetty and Jimmy would talk with some of them. Then we would make the rounds on Montauk. From Gosman's we would drive along the Harbor, then south on Westlake Drive to Star Island, and go across the causeway and onto the small island that sat amid Lake Montauk. There, we would drive to the end of the road near the Coast Guard Station, turn around and drive out, all the while checking out the docks, boats, and the water. Back to Westlake Drive, north to Flamingo Road, turn south and head toward Montauk Village. At the crest of the hill, we would turn west onto Tuthill Road and drive along the high eastern cliffs of Fort Pond Bay.

Fort Pond Bay is a large horseshoe shaped cut on the northern shore of the Montauk peninsula. It is an oceanic embayment open to the north and facing into Block Island Sound, with Culloden Point to the east and Rocky Point to the west. It's depth drops off very quickly from shore and reaches about 50 feet between the two Points of land. That made the Bay suitable for vessels with a deep draft.

On the East End

Fort Pond Bay Vista. A view of the relatively undisturbed southern and western landscape of Fort Pond Bay in 1979. This vista is looking northwesterly from the dunes near Jimmy Lester's east pound net toward Rocky Point and the bluffs rising 80 feet to 100 feet above the Bay. The leader of Jimmy's west pound net can be seen running across the center of the photo, with some gulls sitting atop a few of the leader's stakes.

Occasionally, the Bay served as an overnight refuge or safe haven for the U.S. Coast Guard training barque *Eagle* or a U.S. Navy submarine from New London, Connecticut. Montauk juts out into the ocean some 20 miles from the mainlands of Connecticut and Rhode Island, with open water clear across Block Island Sound.

On a clear day, those mainlands can be seen from the Montauk bluffs. And the East End of Long Island can be seen from the Rhode Island ocean dunes. Montauk thus is a peninsular point of land 20 miles south of the New England coast and 130 miles east of New York City. It still has an island feeling to it.

At a good vantage point high up on the eastern cliffs of Fort Pond Bay, we would stop, and Jimmy would use his field glasses to inspect the water and his fish traps at the southern end of the Bay, west of the old Lab site. Once he was satisfied, we headed south to Montauk Village. He drove the Old Montauk Highway westward along the ocean, checking on the draggers fishing the Backside. Jimmy would stop along the ocean cliffs and point seaward. "There's Scotty's boat and Elisha's, both under tow. Dick Stern's dragging to the west. Tony's haulin' back." I strained with field glasses to read the names on the boats. Jimmy knew them by owner or captain. And by some other means recognizable to him, that even field glasses couldn't help me with. Such a tour of Montauk Harbor and the fishing grounds would get my adrenaline flowing and was worth a long year's wait.

I've seen other baymen behave similarly. Some spring mornings on the ocean beaches, the sea would be too rough and choppy for the haul seiners to make a set. Even when it had been blowing for a day or so and they knew no fishing could be done, several baymen in pickups would be on the beach, just checking it out. Francis and Calvin Lester would be there. And Jimmy's grandfather, "Cap'n Bill." It was their life. They couldn't not be there. They'd pull up to the beach and sit there a while, quietly. The chatter on their CB radios, some from draggers nearshore, some from other seiners farther down the beach, would provide an update on fishing conditions and what was running. Jimmy told me that the guys who were fishing then were the ones who really loved it. The ones who wanted to do nothing else, guys like himself. Fishing was a hard business, not very profitable, good years mixed with bad. What had been a father-son tradition for centuries was changing. Some sons were finding other work. Some fathers discouraged sons from such a shaky business. I'd been hearing such talk for a few years and observing the melancholy among the baymen when they discussed it. It made *me* melancholy.

There's Weather Today

But that day in the mid-1980s, we had weather. Montauk Harbor was slick and glassy, not a breath of wind. We pulled off of West Lake Drive opposite Underwood's Motel and parked in a gravely open space near the water. We walked along a path between the reeds and bulrushes to a small dock where Jimmy tied up his 41-foot Chesapeake

Bay boat *Tern*. The ping of small engines and the roar of large ones could be heard from far across the water. Even the distant voice of a deck hand from an outbound party boat carried over the water in the early morning. Jimmy removed the cover of the engine well on *Tern's* afterdeck and started her up. She started immediately; no cranking, no groaning, no black exhaust. The engine was a clean six-cylinder Ford diesel. *Tern* was used as a pound trap tender and also as a dragger. Some days after tending the traps, Jimmy would spend the remainder of the morning and the afternoon dragging the bottom for fish at some favorite spots in Block Island Sound. I've been Jimmy's crewman many times while dragging there. We would set the net overboard, pay it out to the proper length, and then tow for an hour while we talked. Sometimes we would boil a pot of water on *Tern's* small stove and enjoy a cup of tea while towing.

As *Tern* made her way out of the slip and toward the harbor entrance, I used Jimmy's field glasses to examine the fishing fleet, and my old pocket Instamatic camera to take several pictures. That old camera went everywhere with me when I used to work on Montauk. I literally have thousands of 35mm slides and photographs of my sea exploits aboard several fishing boats and research ships, including *Tern* and Jimmy's sharpies, of course, as well as vessels like R/V *Kyma* and R/V *Albatross*, and the draggers *Lady Barbara* and *Louise*. Aboard those ships, I plied the waters all around Long Island, the South Fork and the East End, Long Island Sound, and the Northwest Atlantic from Montauk Point to Georges Bank. Recently, I've been digitizing those old slides and using them for lectures and school classroom visits. After more than 35 years, they still are useful and educational. Jimmy gave a small "Bonac wave" to some fishermen on the deck of a large dragger, and to the captain of a small charter boat making ready. "H'lo, Cap" was all that was said. A few anglers fished off the west jetty, that was ringed with floating buoys, marking the presence of lobster pots on the bottom. During the summer months, American lobsters move inshore into shallow water from their

Trap Tender and Dragger *Tern*. Bayman Jimmy Lester's Chesapeake Bay-style dragger and work boat *Tern* streaming into Montauk Harbor after a day of tending his pound nets in Fort Pond Bay and trawling for fish in Block Island Sound. A scientist at the helm could be risky business, but during his bottom trawling operations, I would get to take the helm while Jimmy worked the power winches to set and retrieve the net. *Tern* was a good all-purpose fishing boat on which I always felt safe.

deeper offshore wintering areas. They can be caught then by baited traps or pots on the bottom and by trawlers working in nearshore waters.

Once *Tern* was outside the harbor entrance and in Block Island Sound, Jimmy began watching the depth finder, turned to port, and brought *Tern* to a westward course. The engine picked up and we cruised, almost effortlessly, on a calm smooth Block Island Sound sea toward Fort Pond Bay. Still no visible engine exhaust. Only a regular deep hum that I could harmonize with. When diesels are in proper running order and not pushed beyond their efficiency point, they burn clean, visibly. Jimmy throttled up to demonstrate. *Tern* jumped ahead a bit and dark exhaust became visible. Throttle back. No need to hurry and stress the engine. Jimmy kept watch of the depth finder, compass, shoreline, and the waters ahead. Lobster pot buoys were everywhere, all colors and many arrangements. More than I ever remembered seeing during my years working on the East End as a marine biologist. "Why, Jimmy?"

"Well, a lot of guys are fishin' now. Some baymen, and many part-timers and sport fishermen. A lot of guys with just a few pots and not much knowledge. They'll put 'em anywhere; right up next to a commercial fisherman tryin' to make a livin'. Not much room for a boat, certainly not for a dragger. A lot of poachin', too, with guys raidin' others' pots and taking the keeper lobsters. It's nasty business."

That's not the behavior I observed among the baymen toward each other. Sure, they are competitive like anyone working for a living, but they respect each other's property, a person's right to fish, and a privacy about the knowledge of where a baymen just fished and made a good day's wages, and just how much he actually harvested. There seemed to be some community feeling among most of the baymen and their families. When I lived on the East End, I had participated with and helped them in some of their social events, like their annual clam chowder supper at the American Legion hall in Amagansett. It was a fundraiser for the Baymen's Association and open to the public.

The Baymen's Manhattan style chowder was thick, more like a vegetable stew, and very clammy. The best I have ever eaten, bar none. And my wife and I attended the annual dinner and dance sponsored by the Long Island Fishermen's Association. We double dated with Jimmy and his wife. During the monthly Baymen's Association meetings, the formal business meeting was followed by social time and cold brew. A 50–50 raffle was held to raise some money. Tickets were sold for a dollar each, with half of the proceeds going to the Association, the other half to the holder of the winning raffle ticket. I won once and gave my half back to the Association, asking that it be used to support the Association's Newsletter that was being edited and produced by Jimmy's wife Kathi. The baymen really appreciated that support and generosity.

Fishing with Jimmy

Jimmy maneuvered *Tern* easily through the maze of lobster pot buoys and markers. Off of Culloden Point, one eye on the depth finder, one on the compass, and both on the water ahead, Jimmy brought *Tern* to port again and headed sou'westerly into Fort Pond Bay. He did this in the fog one morning, from the Harbor to Fort Pond Bay, and managed to guide *Tern* directly to his traps; using only the depth finder, compass, and some sixth "water" sense that East End baymen possess. Jimmy knew the landscape of the ocean bottom and could traverse it from above with his depth finder, rather like an experienced airplane pilot using "pilotage" to navigate by the landscape and landmarks below.

And then I saw Fort Pond Bay ahead! It had been a while since I was there and I felt a rush of enthusiasm, of adrenaline. I took the field glasses and stepped out on deck. Leaning against the rigging for stability, I scanned the Bay from Culloden Point to Rocky Point. Nothing much had changed, except for the presence of many more pound traps than I remembered. During the early and mid-1970s, Jimmy had the only pound net sets in the Bay. Trap fishing was widespread throughout Gardiner's and Napeague Bays to the west, and had been for centuries, and I believe Jimmy's were the easternmost permanent sets on Long Island at that time.

Fort Pond Bay in the early 1970s was quiet, uncrowded, and solitary. There were only a few vessels regularly seen then in the Bay. The *Perry B* was a lobster boat converted into a private yacht that was moored at Duryea's Dock on the east shore. The Research Vessel *Kyma* had been tied at the Lab's dock on the southern shore during spring through fall, and moved into Montauk Harbor during winter. And, of course, there were Jimmy's boats as he tended his two pound traps on the southern shore just west of the old Lab site.

On the East End

Studying Montauk's Fish Diversity

The marine waters of Fort Pond Bay and Montauk are influenced by the tidal and wind driven currents of the Atlantic Ocean, Long Island and Block Island Sounds, and the Peconic/Gardiner's Bay system as they ebb and flood near and around Montauk Point. That interplay of waters brings a great diversity of marine life to the Montauk area and made the study of fishes there very exciting. East End writer and former commercial fisherman John Cole, in his book *Striper*, called Montauk Point the northern migratory crossroads for migrating striped bass. Many striped bass of the mid-Atlantic coastal migratory stock pass by and around the Point on their way to and from their northerly summer feeding areas in New York, New England, and the southern Canadian marine and estuarine waters.

The fish tagging and return studies that we did at the Lab, with help from Jimmy and the haul seine baymen during the early and mid-1970s, indicated that by mid-July or so, migrating striped bass had reached the extremes of their northerly spring migration. By then, the bass had passed Montauk Point and had taken up summer residence within the Peconic/Gardiner's Bay system, in New York, in the Connecticut waters of Long Island Sound, in Rhode Island, Massachusetts, and Maine. The waters surrounding Montauk are among the best striped bass fishing areas on the entire East Coast, especially during the spring and autumn migrations.

Jimmy and I catalogued 108 fish species caught in Fort Pond Bay, mostly in his traps, from 1970 through 1978. We co-authored five articles in the old *New York Fish and Game Journal*, and one article in *American Currents*, on those captured fishes. That catalogue included a large cubera snapper (*Lutjanus cyanopterus*), 37 inches long weighing 31 pounds, that Jimmy caught and which Byron Young wrote about in the *Fish and Game Journal* in 1978. Byron told me the cubera snapper now resides in the Museum of Natural History in New York City. Jimmy and Byron donated it to the Museum's

Fishing with Jimmy

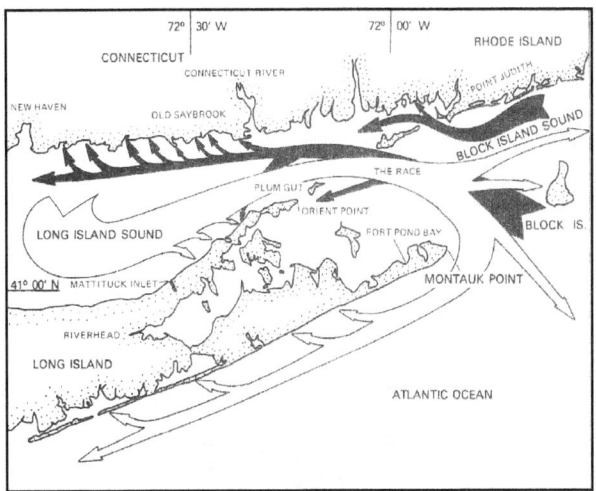

Oceanic Migratory Crossroads. John Cole, in his classic 1978 book *Striper: A Story of Fish and Man*, noted that Montauk Point is the "oceanic migratory crossroads" for striped bass. Part of the reason for this is the interplay of the marine currents, both wind-driven and tide-driven, that gather and move around the Point. This figure (from Hickey, 1981) depicts a stylized and general net flow of the waters, with the bottom water currents (dark arrows) in the spring and the surface water currents (white arrows) in the fall. The longshore water flow and movement of sand along Long Island's ocean beaches is also east to west.

collection. At that time it was the only cubera snapper specimen in the Museum. Jimmy and I also documented two fish species never before reported from New York's marine waters, a horse-eye jack (*Caranx latus*) and a glasseye snapper (*Priacanthus cruentatus*). Jimmy also caught a mature male tarpon (*Megalops atlanticus*) in 1974 that was larger than any previously reported for New York waters. It was 63 inches long and weighed 64 pounds.

A photo of that tarpon, taken by Carl Mamay, made several of the local Long Island newspapers. It was not unusual for the *East Hampton Star* to report on Jimmy's fishing and his catches in Fort Pond Bay. In 2002, New York biologists Phil Briggs and John Waldman compiled an updated listing of all the fishes known to exist

On the East End

Tending the Trap Net. Bayman Jimmy Lester, at right, and crewman Billy Havens lifting the bailing piece of Jimmy's pound nets, or fish traps, in Fort Pond Bay, Montauk, in May 1981. The sharpie in which they are standing is inside the box of the net. The net's leader can be seen on the poles or stakes running toward the beach. Moving or migrating fishes swimming with the currents running parallel to the beach, encounter the leader that extends from the water surface to the Bay bottom. They then must turn seaward in trying to swim around the net that blocks their movements. In doing so, they are diverted into a net funnel that takes them into the box and the bailing piece where they swim alive until the nets are lifted.

in the coastal marine waters of New York State. They annotated 338 fish species and drew upon all of those papers I wrote with Jimmy and other baymen. It is a nice feeling to have contributed to the knowledge of Long Island and local East End fish diversity, abundance, distribution, and seasonality.

As must be obvious, I really liked the opportunity to observe and study the fishes of Fort Pond Bay with Jimmy at his traps, and then to write about the unique and important things we found

Record Tarpon. The author with a tarpon caught during July 1974 by Jimmy Lester in his pound nets in Fort Pond Bay. This fish measured 63 inches in total length and weighed 64 pounds. At that time, it was the largest tarpon ever reported from the waters of the State of New York and was the first one ever recorded as having been captured from the waters of Block Island Sound. During summers, the Gulf Stream comes very close to Montauk and brings with it Caribbean fish species such as tarpon.
Photo by Carl Mamay.

and observed. In fact, his pound nets were wonderful scientific fish sampling devices. They were stationary, never moved, and were in the same location during the entire long fishing season of spring through fall, year after year. They fished undisturbed for at least 24-hour periods, and were tended three to seven days per week, weather depending. During periods of good weather, they generally were tended on a daily basis. They were run consistently by the same operator (Jimmy) in the same manner during every tending. They had a net mesh size between two and six inches and thus usually did not capture small fishes or those small species with elongated body forms, like bay anchovy, Atlantic silversides, or sand lance. The net hauling procedure also allowed the keeper fishes to be sorted from the shorts and unwanted species, which could be released unharmed back to the Bay. I liked being able to return unwanted animals alive and it was a good conservation practice. I had struggled with this in other aspects of my marine fisheries research, so when fishing with Jimmy at his traps, I appreciated being able to do less harm to fishes we caught.

Tending Jimmy's Traps

All of those thoughts ran through me as we cruised toward the west shore of the Bay. We were closer now, and with the glasses I again examined the old Lab site. No boats at the dock. No one fishing there either. Why did I do that? Couldn't I just enjoy the day on the water with my friend?

"Hey, Bub!" Jimmy shouted to me.

"Huh? Oh, time to go to work," I mumbled.

"Grab the boat hook there and get the line on the sharpie when we pull along side."

We had reached the western shore of the Bay, near the old sand and gravel mine, where Jimmy moored his trap boat. It was a small row boat-like craft called a "sharpie," one of the traditional kinds of work boats used by the baymen. Jimmy used it to maneuver inside the pound nets. He built it himself, from scratch. I had watched him do some of it in the large out building and work shed (that he also built) in his back yard. Baymen are jacks-of-all-marine-trades, very self-reliant. Jimmy was a good mechanic, carpenter, welder, and boat builder. One winter he even had *Tern* up on blocks in his back yard with the transom up next to his out building. He rebuilt and reshaped the transom to suit his fishing needs. Jimmy was very interested in all kinds of fishing boats. I think he got fishing and boat ideas from observing them. I recall his interest in the kind of traditional work boats that were used on Barnegat Bay, New Jersey, boats similar to his sharpie. Jimmy and his family visited us in the winter of 1976, when we lived in Forked River, NJ, after I left the East End.

For a few months, I worked for an environmental consulting company studying the marine ecology and fisheries of Barnegat Bay. We took Jimmy to the harbor of Forked River (pronounced as "FORK-ed" River) where he found and identified several garvies. The garvey

Fishing with Jimmy

To Catch Fish, Come to Montauk, Long Island, N.Y.

Bring in the Fish. Jimmy Lester sent me this postcard in 1979. The printed description on the card says "This is a view from the Montauk Marine Basin showing some of the boats that bring in the fish." *Tern* is right in the middle of the photo, but it is not rigged for commercial fishing as when Jimmy fished with her. There is no outside ship's wheel, throttle, or power winch. The transom appears to be square. After Jimmy purchased *Tern*, he trailered her home, put her up on blocks in his back yard, and rebuilt the transom which he extended and rounded. (Wonder if the wheelhouse leaked before Jimmy had her?)

was an open work boat that looked a lot like a sharpie, except larger. They were used by the local New Jersey baymen for clamming and fishing on Barnegat Bay. Some of the garvies were outfitted with large V-8 engines and long upright vertical exhaust pipes on their afterdecks. The exhaust pipes had metal buckets laying over them in the harbor to keep the rain out. I heard local stories about some of those garvies being able to outrun the conservation wardens and bay constables. Aside from that, those garvies looked like sturdy and durable bay work boats.

On the East End

At Jimmy's traps that morning, I hooked the mooring line on his sharpie and Jimmy fastened it to a cleat on *Tern*. Slowly, *Tern* made her way, towing the sharpie, to Jimmy's "east trap," that ran off the southern beach not far from the Port Royal Motel. He had two traps there about a quarter mile apart. From the beach off Navy Road, you could practically reach out and touch the shoreward end of the "leader," that part of the net "system" running perpendicular to the beach. The leader blocks the alongshore movement of fishes and "leads" them offshore and into the inner pounds of the trap, and then into the "box," at the seaward end, where they are trapped alive. *Tern* was maneuvered among the anchor lines that held the trap net in place and then Jimmy tied her to the wooden stakes along the seaward edge of the box, the hexagonal shaped outermost section of the net that holds the entrapped fishes alive.

I smiled, remembering how many times I had been in this very spot on a Lab-owned boat, while observing Jimmy's catch and tagging fishes there. One time, I was in a 12-foot rowboat with Walt Job. We rowed to Jimmy's traps from the Lab dock. Many times I motored to the traps in a slick 17-foot Boston Whaler (yes, a plastic boat). And once on a 26-foot cabin cruiser the Lab had for a while, that we scientists tried to put astern between the anchor lines. Jimmy still talks about that, and the worry, with three scientists on a plastic boat, trying not to destroy his nets.

"See anything, Bub?" Jimmy called from the wheelhouse as he cut off the engine.

"Yes, yes. Skates, dogfish, sea robins, horsefeet, and spider crabs," I answered with a smile. All were nuisance species to the baymen as they were not of any market value then, and often required extra work to untangle from the nets.

"Damn scien'ists," was all Jimmy uttered under his breath.

Skates and Bad Luck. The author standing in a sharpie inside the pound-net box and holding two live species of skate caught in one of Jimmy Lester's trap nets in Fort Pond Bay in 1977. To the left is a little skate (*Raja erinacea*) and to the right is a clearnose skate (*Raja eglanteria*). Skates even seemed to have personality, as they are flexing upward here, seemingly to be photographed. They went back into the Bay. Over the years, Jimmy and I recorded 13 species of skates and their relatives, the sharks and rays, from Fort Pond Bay. I am wearing yellow oilers, which Jimmy said was bad luck on a boat. Jimmy always wore black.

I had been hanging over the port rail looking down into the net. Jimmy joined me, briefly, and then pulled the sharpie up to the transom. He motioned and we both stepped in. He maneuvered the sharpie hand-over-hand, using the ropes and stakes that supported the amazing (and confusing) array of twine on the trap net. First, he released two lines to collapse the underwater funnel that leads from the inner pounds and into the box. Fishes swimming along shore encounter the leader, turn and swim offshore in an attempt to go around it. In doing so, they encounter the inner pounds or wings of the net system that guides them to the funnel and into the box, where they are trapped alive. Then we went from side to side, and back again, around the box pulling up the twine and adjusting this line and that. We were raising up the box so that the fish inside would be concentrated at the seaward edge in the "bailing piece," near where *Tern* was tied, so we could scoop them out onto *Tern*'s deck. When all of the adjustments were made, Jimmy released a line that opened up the shoreward side of the box, at the water line, and we pulled the sharpie inside.

We worked the twine some more from the inside of the box and moved the trapped fishes into the bailing piece. And then the excitement began. Concentrated into the smaller and shallower space of the bailing piece, the fishes became excited and nervous. So did Jimmy. The water appeared to boil from the thrashing fishes. Boston mackerel darted across and through the mass with a green flash. Blackback flounder and fluke were beneath. Bunkers were mixed in. Scup, also called porgies, of several sizes were plentiful. Most of the other fish species tended to be all about the same size within a species group, like the mackerel, all about 12 inches long. But several size and age groups of scup were there. Several spirited striped bass thrashed about. And a nice bunch of loligo squid near the bottom of the bailing piece.

Lots of searobins were moving slowly, almost cautiously, together throughout. They are pretty fish, with their wing-like pectoral fins extended as they swim slowly and gracefully, making them appear to be flying through the water. They were not a sought after fish and had very little market value. But robins are good eating, especially on the grill. Such a handsome, tasty, and abundant fish deserved more respect, I thought. Jimmy occasionally caught a nice haul of striped bass, but he didn't rely on bass only. His traps caught a nice diversity of marine life, and he would count on the diversity for its market value. Loligo squid and butterfish could be a valuable catch, especially when they were moving into the bays during spring. Jimmy's traps being the most easterly on the South Fork sometimes would bring him the first good harvest of some species, and thus a nice day's pay at the market.

One lone lobster was there that day, along with a few dogfish sharks, some horseshoe crabs (called "horsefeet" locally), a dozen or so skates, and a mess of spider crabs all would get in the way of sorting out the keepers, but they would be returned to the Bay alive. All in all it was not a banner day, but I expected that this harvest and that from his west trap might pay Jimmy's expenses. I was strictly volunteer help, being "paid" with fisheries data and a nice day on the water with my friend. Jimmy offered me a share of the day's profits a few years earlier, but I declined. I wasn't along for profit. He was the seafood producer I was the happy amateur bayman.

What that day did do was far more than pay expenses, however. It lifted spirits and erased troubles. The old Lab was the farthest thing from my mind. I renewed acquaintances with many old comrades of the sea. I wrestled with a ten-pound fluke. Tried to hold onto a spirited and powerful mackerel. Picked up a horseshoe crab by the tail and examined its underside, trying to remember those anatomical parts from Marine Bio 501. [I had cleared the surf of swimmers at Jones Beach, one summer day in the late 1960s, when I picked up a live horseshoe crab by the tail and held it up above my head. The swimmers all screeched as they headed for the beach. It was wonderful]. I was squirted all over by squid ink, on the foul weather gear, face, and glasses. Grabbed by that lobster. Scup spines to the fingers. Needles and jabs from Jimmy.

And Jimmy, he was spirited, busy, and smiling, unlike the man I had seen a few years earlier. His wife Kathi was ill for some time with an undefined respiratory ailment. She died in 1981. His father, William T. Lester, a respected bayman once robust and full of life, had emphysema and spent much time at rest with a supply of bottled oxygen. His son was nearly grown and finishing high school. Jimmy had recently purchased *Tern*, and fishing, along with income, had been spotty the past year or two. He felt all of those pressures, and I could see it in his nervous manner at home. But on the water, things were different. Jimmy told me that when he was at his traps, catching those fish, everything was OK. There, he had no cares.

Like the difference between a gull walking on the beach watching for signs of danger, and one soaring carelessly and effortlessly on the safety of the sea winds above. I could see the different Jimmy Lester standing in the sharpie inside that trap net. And I understood what he said. As a teenager and college student in the 1960s, I very often found myself on the Jersey shores, usually Ocean City, escaping the pressures of peers, parents, and a changing and troubled America I did not really understand. The ocean environment called to me, yes it did. And I went, and walked the beaches, slept on the beaches, ate on the beaches. I breathed a salt air that I still can smell. The ocean air of day was scented with the smells of the vast salt marshes by night. There is no greater more refreshing smell than the wind across a natural salt marsh. My father died in November of 1974. In the spring of '75 the Lab put me on notice and I departed that summer. I recall spending a lot of time on the ocean beaches of the East End then, mostly around Indian Wells. And much time at Louse Point overlooking Bonac Creek and breathing its marsh-laden air. Louse Point was my friend. The winter was best. Hard winds, white caps, gulls, few people. At the water, I was OK.

Fun, Educational, Never Dull

Fishing with Jimmy was fun. I got to help a lot. That day in the mid-1980s, like so many others before, I *was* the help. After the catch was concentrated into the bailing piece, we stepped back onto *Tern*. Jimmy started the engine (yes, yes; it fired right up) and engaged the power take-off. He showed me how to use the "h'ister" (the capstan head, with block and tackle) to help lift a large scoop net full of fish that he would operate from the sharpie. He stepped back into the trap boat and we proceeded to empty the bailing piece, scoop after scoop, onto *Tern*'s afterdeck.

The operation went very smoothly, and I had time to sort through the catch while Jimmy tended to resetting the trap, hand-over-hand, this line and that. By the time he reset the funnel, I had sorted all of the keepers into bushel baskets, and returned to the Bay all of the shorts of species for which there were state-mandated minimum legal size lengths (species like fluke, flounder, striped bass, scup). Most

Good Day's Harvest. I was fishing with Jimmy in November 1975, during one of my return visits to the East End, when he caught this 34-pound striped bass in his trap net. It was the largest bass he had ever caught. On that day his two pound nets yielded almost 800 pounds of striped bass from Fort Pond Bay. Jimmy would catch striped bass occasionally, but that day was an especially good harvest that came as a result of a northerly wind that brought the current and the bass into Fort Pond Bay. During the fall, striped bass migrate from New England and Long Island Sound and move around Montauk Point on their southerly journey to natal waters elsewhere. After that day's harvest, Jimmy said that I was good luck. My memories of fishing on the East End are forever bright and fresh. Thanks, Cap.

of the spider crabs were dumped out of the bailing piece en masse after it had been emptied of everything else. I liked the part about returning unusable, undesirable, or undersized animals to the sea. I recall watching intently as a small scup was returned; it paused briefly at the surface, and then darted downward and out of sight with a burst of energy.

I really got Jimmy's Bonac ire up one time, though, a few years before. We were tending the trap. It was mostly full of crabs and small dogfish sharks; not many keepers. One smooth dogfish was a full-grown female, about three feet long, plump and round with pups. Smooth dogs are "viviparous" with a placental connection between the embryonic pups and the mother. When born, the pups are fully formed and resemble small adults. Dogfish, however, generally were a fisherman's nemesis then. Not much value, if any, at the market. And they could just destroy trawls and gill nets by twisting and turning inside them, specially the spiny dogfish species with their stiff and spiny fins, so that they get as bound up in the net as bubble gum can in a little boy's hair. On *Tern*'s deck, the female smooth dogfish began wriggling and writhing, as if in labor. So I picked her up, held her tail-down over the outside rail, and stroked her belly downward. After a few firm strokes, out came a pup; slender and gray, about 12 inches long. Plop, into the Bay. It paused, and swam slowly down and out of sight. I still can see it.

I called out, "Hey, Jimmy! Did you see that? Watch!" Stroke. Stroke. Stroke. Plop. Pause. Swim.

"Huh?"

Stroke. Stroke. Plop.

Stroke. Stroke. Plop.

"Those are **dogs**, Bub!"

"Yeah! Ever seen this done before?"

Stroke. Stroke. Plop.

"Dogs? Who *needs* 'em? How 'bout tryin' that big fluke there?"

Stroke. Stroke. Plop.

"Damn scien'ists."

After the east trap was reset, we moved over to the west trap, about a thousand feet away, and repeated the operation. The day's harvest was taken back to Montauk Harbor for icing and shipment to Market.

Fishing with Jimmy

I was always impressed by the way Jimmy treated his harvest, once on board the boat. Fishes were sorted by species into separate baskets. Flukes and flounders were placed with the light underside up, so that as the fish's body fluids settled, the clean-looking underside would not become discolored. Cared-for fish are more attractive to the market customer and sometimes brought a better price to both retailer and fisherman.

Bay water would be used to rinse and clean the harvest. Ice, from a large onboard ice chest at *Tern*'s transom, would be added to the baskets, as needed. Canvass tarps were placed over the entire iced harvest to protect them from the sun. Bay water would be flushed across the tarps periodically, to keep the harvest cool and fresh. Once at the packing house in the harbor, Jimmy carefully weighed each species group and placed them into waxed cartons, with plenty of ice, for transport to distant markets. A written record was made of the harvest, without the use of a scientific clipboard. That done, *Tern* was maneuvered to her mooring. We cleaned up the deck and then headed for a late breakfast at Salivar's Restaurant in the Harbor, my treat.

Jimmy had not always fished with *Tern*. She was acquired during the late 1970s, after I had left Montauk. When I was working with Jimmy and tagging fish at his traps in the early 1970s, Jimmy used two sharpies, one with an outboard motor and one towed behind that was used as the trap boat. The motorized boat was kept at launching site on the western shore of Fort Pond bay and launched there. Jimmy then motored to the trap boat moored offshore, put it in tow, and proceeded to the traps. Sometimes I would ride in the trap boat and bail out the rainwater on the way. Tending the nets was the same, but all of the bailing was by hand, with smaller scoop nets than used on *Tern* with her power winch. I recall many a sore back and shoulders from mornings of bailing fishes. And it was a little frustrating on those days when most of the efforts went to returning searobins and crabs, with few keepers. But Jimmy had managed his small business well enough to have his own boat. Sore backs are less frequent, and dragging in Block Island Sound added another dimension to his life on the water. With *Tern*, Jimmy could tend his traps and drag, and with sharpies he also could work the inner bays and shallow waters for scallops and other quarries. Way t' go, Cap!

Jimmy was a scallop fisher also. He had a small working shop as part of the out building in his back yard where he would open the fresh bay scallops he caught each day. The scallop shop was maybe six feet by eight or ten feet, not large, but very functional. There were windows for natural light, electric lighting for night work, a concrete floor with a drain, a working counter, sink, and a refrigerator. Jimmy would bring the scallops he had just dredged from the bays into his shop for "opening."

All in seemingly one smooth motion, Jimmy would open the scallops using a special small opening knife that he pushed into the scallop between the upper and lower shells. Then he would slit the one adductor muscle that the scallop uses to open and close those two shells, and cut out that muscle which is the edible meat part of the scallop. Then, all in that same smooth motion, Jimmy would scoop out the severed muscle with the knife and then flick it with his thumb up into the air and into a bowl nearby on the counter. Sometimes he did this so fast, with so many scallops, that he didn't appear to even look in the direction of the bowl. He just flipped the edible meats into the air, never missing the bowl! Then they went into the refrigerator before he took them to market for sale. From building boats, repairing engines, welding metal scallop dredges, making nets, navigating in the fog, to flipping scallop meats like tiddlywinks. That was the versatility of an East End bayman.

Fishing with Jimmy was educational. I learned a lot. Like how to tell, from Amagansett, if the wind was blowing too hard to tend the fish traps on Montauk. First thing when you get up in the morning,

Fishing with Jimmy

Heading to the Trap. When I fished with Jimmy Lester in the early 1970s, he used a sharpie to motor to his trap nets in Fort Pond Bay. Here, we are heading easterly on the Bay, into the rising early morning sun, with a second sharpie in tow that was used inside the nets and to hold the harvest. Jimmy is in the front boat, and I am in the trailing boat. I was his crew and deck hand many times, bailing the boat of rain water, lifting the nets, bailing the fishes, sorting the harvest, returning unwanted animals to the Bay, transferring the harvest to his truck on shore, and then packing and icing the harvest for shipment at Montauk Harbor.

When he purchased and fished with *Tern* in later years, I would help moor *Tern* at the docks and then clean her up for another day's work. In between all that work, I measured and tagged several species of fishes for movement and migration studies, and kept records of unusual animals we caught. One winter flounder I tagged was caught and released by Jimmy six times. It never left Fort Pond Bay and Jimmy remarked that he knew the fish personally. It was a nice legal-sized fish, so on the seventh capture, Jimmy'd had enough. It went to market.

check the toilet. If the water in the bowl is moving, sloshing, you don't have weather. Hard winds across the plumbing vent pipe on the roof will change the pressure inside the whole pipe system, and slosh the water. Try it, and then go back to bed.

Then there's seafood cookery. The best fish I ever ate was cooked on the hot muffler of a fishing boat while working on the water. Jimmy had served as crew on an offshore dragger some years earlier (on Bruce Erickson's boat, *Marge E*, I think) and learned that fish right out of the trawl, wrapped in tin foil (especially with lemon and butter), and placed on the top of the upright hot muffler, would cook up just fine. He told me this when I was working at the Lab on Montauk, so I took the foil on a sampling cruise aboard a small dragger that the Lab chartered for fish sampling on Long Island Sound, the dragger *Lady Barbara*. We caught some whiting (silver hake) by trawl in Long Island Sound, so I removed the head and entrails from one, wrapped the fish in foil and placed it on the muffler, which stood on the afterdeck, upright, next to the wheelhouse. After ten minutes or so, the foil package swelled a bit and steam leaked from the folds. And good?! Finest kind, Bub!.

You've heard of corn coming off the stalk and into the pot. Well, fish on the muffler is the only thing fresher. I was so impressed with that deck-side culinary procedure that I wrote it up as a recipe for a cookbook that one of my professional scientific associations, the American Fisheries Society, was developing. My procedure and recipe for "fish on the muffler" was published by the Society in 1991 in its *Sea Fare Cookbook*. The baymen are, in general, the best sources of seafood dinners. They are particular about what they eat and how it is prepared. Jimmy's was the best place in town that my wife and I ever found. Fish, squid, scallops, even skate wings were wonderful! If you want a good seafood restaurant, ask the baymen where they go to eat. Nine out of ten times they will say "home." But if you can

Tern's **Wheelhouse.** Captain Jimmy Lester is piloting *Tern* in her wheelhouse (which only leaks when it rains) on Block Island Sound. Jimmy also could pilot *Tern* from the afterdeck using the ship's wheel on the outside of the wheelhouse and the throttle next to it. Those outside controls allowed Jimmy to pilot the boat while setting and retrieving a bottom trawl using the power winch just below the ship's wheel. Dragging thus could be a one-man operation. The blue barrel at the lower right was used to hold interesting fishes and other sea creatures alive. The hose running into it supplied fresh seawater.

We sometimes would put into that barrel those unusual fishes we caught that we eventually wrote about for the *New York Fish and Game Journal*. One morning when I boarded *Tern*, there were two lumpfish (*Cyclopterus lumpus*), a male and a female, in the barrel from the day before. They had been in the pound net and Jimmy kept them alive because he knew I would like to see them. Lumpfish are beautiful animals and Jimmy would catch them now and then in his pound nets during spring.

squeeze out the tenth (like I did those dogfish pups), you'll find a good local place to eat.

Fishing with Jimmy was never dull. We laughed a lot. He kidded me about being a scientist (plastic boats, clipboards, and so on). And

On the East End

I asked him, on every trip, about the leak in the roof of *Tern's* wheelhouse.

"Is it patched yet?"

"No. Only leaks when it rains," was the standard response.

We could sit in his kitchen and talk for hours about fishing. About anything related to fishing or the water. Like the time I revived and freed a stunned blowfish that had been dropped by a gull from a height of about 50 feet onto the beach. That stupid bird must have thought it was a clam. One night amidst such talk, Jimmy became very serious and spoke quietly. About a gull that was visiting his traps.

"Now don't tell anyone this," Jimmy said. "I've never told anyone but my wife. There's this gull that comes to my trap. He sits up on a stake watching, when I'm inside the box … and he talks."

As he related this, Jimmy looked away, a little embarrassed, a little tickled by it.

"He says 'H'lo' in a high scratchy voice like a parrot. And I say 'H'lo' back and throw him a butterfish." Gulls love butterfish. Gulls love anything that's a free meal.

Jimmy expected, I think, that I wouldn't believe him. That a scientist from the Lab would find this silly. Those Posey Lesters, you know. I heard the story several more times. "He was there today. Why the @#$%& doesn't he come when you're there?"

Well he did, finally. One morning, Jimmy and I were inside the box of his trap net scooping out the bailing piece, when a gull came and alighted atop a wooden trap stake. There were lots of gulls around fish traps and fishing boats, I liked watching them, always. They're nosey, brash, noisy, sleek, splendid flyers, part of the coast. One more gull at the traps wasn't even noticed. Until ….

"H'lo," said a high pitched parrot-like voice.

"H'lo," Jimmy answered, very calmly. He looked at me, and I at him, both of us smiling. Jimmy reached down for a butterfish and gently tossed it at the gull. Gulp. Swallow. Gulls do not taste their food, just swallow. Satisfaction was on Jimmy's face.

"H'lo," came the voice from on high again.

"H'lo," came the answer.

Toss. Gulp. Swallow.

Hey, I'm sorry, Jimmy. You know I never doubted you. So forgive me for telling this one. I know that you kept the talking gull story to yourself. I also remember that horse-eye jack you caught in the summer of 1973. Just a little guy. And not in any records or books of fishes known from New York's marine waters. But you knew what it was, having never seen one before. I had to search that fine Lab library for a book that would confirm its identity, you know we scientists like proof. But I didn't doubt you. Say, ... how did you do that?

Sometime in the latter 1980s, Jimmy met Sandy King Vorpahl, a wonderful person and savvy local baywoman, a Bonacker. She even tolerates Jimmy's eccentric scien'ist friends. They both are fishers for all seasons and very lucky to have found each other.

Fishing with Jimmy and Sandy, as the Bonackers say, is "finest kind."

4

On the Sound

My adventures working with Jimmy at his pound nets in Fort Pond Bay and with the haul seiners on the Atlantic Ocean beaches of the East End were done in between my main fisheries research responsibilities at the Ocean Science Lab on Montauk. It was on Long Island Sound that I was involved in the Montauk Lab's marine environmental contract work for Long Island Lighting Company (LILCO), and its grant work for the New York State DEC, the Army Corps of Engineers, and other agencies. Providing independent marine environmental consulting services to those local organizations was an important aspect of the Lab's work and its life. Those marine environmental monitoring and research activities were conducted all around Long Island, from the Rockaways at the Island's western end, in the ocean off northern New Jersey, to Block Island Sound to the east, the Peconic and Gardiner's Bays on the East End, and the length and breadth of Long Island Sound.

Long Island Sound was a wonderful outdoor lab and classroom that offered me opportunities to meet some influential Long Island fishermen, test my seamanship, observe beautiful and lively fishes, and hone my ethics in the catching, handling and sampling of many thousands of those fishes. I worked onboard the Montauk Lab's oceanographic Research Vessel *Kyma*, as well as onboard a sturdy dragger, *Lady Barbara*, owned and operated by a sturdy and salty commercial fisherman from central Long Island. My time at sea on the Sound gave me an appreciation for the work and dangers that commercial fisherman face every day. I shared many of my experiences on the Sound with the East End baymen, who could identify with all of them. On the Sound I came to realize that I needed to reduce the number of fishes I was catching and killing for science. My environmental ethics were put to the test and given a new shot in the arm. I shared those ethical dilemmas with my scientific colleagues, and I continue to share them with students at every opportunity.

The Sound is a large body of marine and estuarine water slightly more than 100 miles long, and 17 miles wide in its central basin. It was carved by the advancing glaciers thirty thousand years ago. When the glaciers' southerly advance came to a stop, they left their rocky debris as ridges of moraines stretching easterly from Queens to Orient Point and Montauk. From Orient, one submerged moraine ridge runs to the coast of Connecticut and Rhode Island and then to Cape Cod. From Montauk, a second ridge runs to Block Island and then on to Martha's Vineyard and Nantucket. The outwash plains of glacial till surrounding the moraines form the bulk of the land mass that is Long Island. The marine basin that now is between Long Island and the mainland of Connecticut and Rhode Island is Long Island Sound.

Kyma

Many of the Long Island Sound marine studies I participated in were conducted aboard the Research Vessel *Kyma* (pronounced as KEY-muh), the mainstay of the Montauk Lab's fleet of boats. She was well suited to coastal and estuarine research work on Long Island, as she was small enough to ply the nearshore and bay waters, and sturdy enough to sample at depths of 100–200 feet in the eastern waters of Long Island and Block Island Sounds. *Kyma* was a 65-foot, 100 ton, diesel powered and converted Army "T" boat, leased by the Lab. She had been a cargo vessel that saw service during the Korean War, and had her hold outfitted as a seagoing laboratory. She was converted to a research vessel by the Office of Naval Research for the National Oceanographic and Atmospheric Administration (NOAA). *Kyma* was rigged for a full range of oceanographic work, including multi-depth water and plankton sampling, collection of bottom sediments and bottom dwelling marine organisms, and trawling for fishes.

Kyma had a large after cabin that functioned as galley, ward room, sleeping quarters, and meeting place at sea for the crew. The captain's quarters were below decks, and forward at the bow, in the forecastle (spelled as fo'c's'le and pronounced as FOKE-sull). *Kyma* could house several scientists and ship's crew in relative comfort (if that really exists at sea) for a several days. In rough seas *Kyma* heaved a lot like the empty old cargo vessel she was, and so did I several times on Block Island Sound. *Kyma* is a Greek work meaning "wave" (as in ocean wave), but I recall one Lab technician insisting that *Kyma* actually meant "Great Wallowing Mother," in deference to her behavior in rough seas.

Kyma would make about eight knots maximum, which meant that steaming time for some sampling trips from Montauk into central and western Long Island Sound took the better part of a day. Steaming through the Race at the Sound's eastern end always was exciting. During the ebbing and flooding tides, the water velocity in the Race

On the East End

The Research Vessel *Kyma*. *Kyma* is approaching the New York Ocean Science Laboratory dock on Fort Pond Bay, Montauk, in the early 1970s. *Kyma* was 65 feet long, displaced 100 tons of water, with a draft of five feet. Originally, she was a Korean War vintage Army "T-boat" — a small cargo vessel that transported materials from larger vessels moored offshore to the inshore harbors and docks. Her below decks cargo holds were converted into a small oceanography laboratory for processing water chemistry and marine biological samples at sea. She was a handsome vessel. *Kyma* (pronounced as KEY-muh) is a Greek word meaning "wave," as in ocean wave. The fact that *Kyma* was a converted cargo vessel made her perform like an empty cargo vessel in rough seas. Many a Lab scientist, even seasoned maritime veterans, experienced seasickness aboard *Kyma*, prompting one scientist to insist that the Greek work Kyma actually translated as "great wallowing mother."

could be four to more than five knots, with the ebbing tide swifter than the flooding tide. With an eight knot capability, I recall *Kyma* steaming through the Race, against the tide, at what seemed like a doggy paddle of a crawl. It could be very treacherous with high seas during the tidal exchanges between Long Island and Block Island Sounds moving through the Race. Before entering the Race, *Kyma*'s

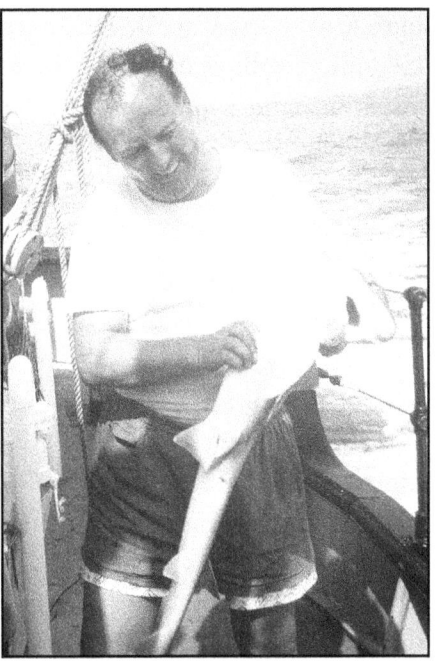

Sandy and Friend. Engineer, first mate, and ship's cook Sandy McLeod holding a smooth dogfish shark caught with bottom trawl by R/V *Kyma*. No, this one did not go into the stewpot, it was returned to sea alive. This dogfish is like the one I "aided in birthing her pups" at Jimmy Lester's trap net on Montauk. Dogfish were common seasonal inhabitants of Long Island waters and very important in the ecosystem. Some fishermen believe that when the dogfishes are numerous and abundant on the sea bottom, they force out other species of commercial value. The smooth dogfish shown here is about three-feet long and full grown. They do not have long pointy sharp teeth that are typically associated with the larger shark species. Dogfish have low flat ridges of teeth for breaking the shells of crabs and other shellfish and for grinding their food. One species of dogfish, the spiny dogfish, has very sharp spines associated with the fins that can puncture a human's skin, otherwise, dogfish are harmless to people.

skipper always put the crew on notice to be watchful, careful, and to stay inside. Those journeys through the Race helped me to appreciate the perils and the stamina of migratory fishes like striped bass that moved through those eastern passages of Long Island during their annual migrations along the East Coast.

The first skipper of *Kyma* whom I knew was an Aussie named Ian McDonald. A fine master was he, and a genuine character. He loved to show the mostly landlubbing scientific staff who was tougher at sea. Ian was at his best during sampling cruises on rough seas on Block Island Sound. On one such late winter cruise the scientific crew was on deck trying to manage sampling, data recording, and balance as *Kyma* rolled and listed without stop. Stomachs became queasy and knees weak. In the wheelhouse, the ship's master filled his mouth with rice krispies, flung open the starboard door to draw attention, and leaned out spewing the cereal with a loud guttural belch, feigning seasickness, that worst of all states-of-being. Satisfied, he calmly returned to the wheel with his infectious Aussie grin, while the rest on board turned to the rail.

Kyma's crew in the early 1970s consisted of her master and an engineer named Sandy McLeod. He, too, qualified for character status, and had a real touch for repairing, nursing, and otherwise keeping *Kyma* shipshape and afloat. He also served as deck hand, mate, and ship's steward (the cook). Roast fowl was his specialty at sea. How he managed this I still do not fully understand. During the worst of weather and sea states, Sandy would quickly prepare a large bird for dinner and put it into the oven. It would endure the worst of conditions and could be heard sliding about in *Kyma*'s oven throughout the day. But they were delicious! At day's end, either on the water steaming homeward, or berthed at an overnight safe harbor, we would delight in the culinary results of Sandy's bird and *Kyma*'s self-basting oven. Ship's master, mate, and scientific crew would sit around the galley table enjoying good fare and much esprit. Nothing lifted spirits at sea, especially after a long day in rough weather, like a good hot meal around the galley table where all can laugh and joke and finally relax.

One of the Lab's first independent environmental consulting activities was an environmental impact assessment contract for Long Island Lighting Company (LILCO) at its Northport power station. Northport was located in the central basin of the Sound a few miles southeast of Eaton's Neck. Two fossil fueled electric generating units were operating at the site then, and a third was being built. We were studying the Sound bottom and the bottom dwelling marine biota in relation to cooling water being pumped through the power station and the thermal effluents being discharged back into the Sound.

Kyma was used for most of the oceanographic and bottom sampling work.

On one of the sampling cruises I steamed from Montauk to Northport onboard *Kyma*, a run of about eight hours. *Kyma*'s master at that time (after Ian McDonald) was a man named George Sandberg, an oceanographer and merchant seaman, who I believe also held a naval commission. George was a fine fellow, likable guy, and good skipper. I enjoyed being in the wheelhouse with George at the helm. He would explain much and even let me help occasionally. At one point during the long run to Northport, Sandy was in the engine room, George and I in the wheelhouse. George needed to go to the head and asked me to take the wheel for a minute. The wind was blowing hard and the seas were sloppy.

"Just hold her at 270°, due west," he said. "I'll be right back." Easy enough, I thought, but in sloppy seas *Kyma* rolled a lot, and the bow moved quite a bit back and forth off of 270°. I should have left well enough alone. Each time she strayed off course, I tried to correct her just as I would have with my car on a windy Long Island Expressway. Each try at correction, however, was met with wind and seas that took *Kyma* right past 270° in the other direction. And with each try the error grew greater and greater. My brow moistened.

"Just get it back to 270°," I thought, "before George returns. Come on, *Kyma*! Great Wallowing Mother is right!" And poor George! The ship's head was a small compartment located near midship on the starboard side of the aftercabin. With all of *Kyma*'s rolling and my unable seamanship, I just knew George was flailing about in the head trying desperately to hit his mark, while I tried desperately to hold mine. By some amazing coincidence, when George returned to the helm, *Kyma* was on 270°, she must have been en route from 180° to 360° at the time. So I quietly stepped aside, while George took the wheel. Nothing was said. I slipped out the starboard door into the cool night air.

A few years later, the Lab had financial difficulties and problems staffing a crew for *Kyma*. She eventually fell into disrepair. I moved to Maryland in the late 1970s. While scanning the May 1985 issue of *Fisheries* magazine, I came across an article on the NOAA Sandy Hook Laboratory. It had a picture of *Kyma*, all clean and shiny, and still rigged for inshore work by its NOAA owners. The old girl was still in business! And so was I. Neither of us were on Montauk. Both had a few more years and some new rigging. My picture was in the same issue of that magazine, as I was an officer with a local Maryland chapter of the American Fisheries Society, which published the magazine. I wondered, if *Kyma* could think, would she remember me? I certainly won't forget her, for our times together were the heights and depths of life at sea. She was retired from government service and marine research work in 1997. I hung on until retirement in 2005.

Lady Barbara

A local commercial fisherman from Port Jefferson, and his small dragger *Lady Barbara*, were chartered by the Montauk Lab as bottom trawler, gill netter, and fish plankton sampler for several of the Long Island Sound marine ecology projects on which I participated. One such study was a small environmental consulting project conducted by the Lab under contract to LILCO in the western basin of the Sound. LILCO had proposed to lay some underwater cable as an electricity "inter-tie" connection with Consolidated Edison of New York. The project involved the sampling of the bottom sediment types and bottom dwelling marine life in the area of the proposed inter-tie so that the environmental impact of the project could be evaluated.

The area we studied was between Sands Point on the south shore of the Sound and New Rochelle on the north shore of the small western basin. We sampled using a Petersen grab, which is a

On the Sound

Hard Working Lady. The dragger *Lady Barbara* was a western-rigged fishing boat with the wheelhouse toward the bow. She was a "side trawler" that used a movable boom to set the bottom trawl over the side from amidships rather than from the stern. The *Lady* could use a bottom grab to study the organisms that lived on the bottom of the Sound, tow a trawl for bottom fishes, set gill nets to capture swimming pelagic fishes, or take water samples. We worked the entire Sound aboard *Lady Barbara*. For the years that we used her for studying the Sound, *Lady Barbara* functioned more as a small research vessel than as a dragger. She was a day fisher, going out early in the morning and sometimes not returning until after dark. *Lady Barbara*, her skipper, and we biologists were a good team of marine samplers and fishers.

device resembling a clamshell dredge used for dredging and filling of bulkhead areas, but much smaller. The grab was lowered with jaws open, its heavy weight causing it to sink several inches into the Sound bottom. Using the hydraulic winch aboard *Lady Barbara* to retrieve it caused the grab to close and take a bite of the bottom. Once on board ship, the grab was opened and its contents placed into a container for transport back to the Lab for study and analysis. *Lady Barbara*, a 43-foot western rigged dragger, was owned by Jim Miller of (oddly enough) Miller Place, near Port Jefferson where the boat was berthed. *Lady Barbara*, named for Jim Miller's wife, was chartered by the Lab and proved to be one of the high points of my time as a marine biologist on the East End. *Lady Barbara* was a main

On the East End

Captain Miller. Fisherman and Captain Jim Miller is running *Lady Barbara*'s power winch to set and retrieve the bottom trawl in Long Island Sound in 1972. I stepped out from the wheelhouse to snap this photo with my trusty Instamatic camera. Jim often gave me the wheel, and verbal instruction along the way, while he did the more dangerous job of operating the winch and the trawl. We had a nice partnership, waterman and biologists. During one ecological study in the Sound in 1973, we caught 59 species of fishes by trawl, and by gill net and beach seine. The *Lady*'s upright muffler is visible at the extreme right of the photo. I used the top flat surface of the hot muffler as a griddle to cook fish, taken right out of the trawl and wrapped in tin foil, then placed on the muffler. "Some good," Bub.

source of my "ship time" for a few years while we were studying fishes and marine life at several locations on the Sound.

Jim Miller was a seasoned waterman and skipper and I often marveled at how he could handle and maneuver *Lady Barbara* between and among the myriad of lobster pot buoys and around the rocks in the western Sound. Our sampling transect for the LILCO "inter-tie" project, from Sands Point, took us to the Execution Rocks island in the middle of the western Sound, where sampling was very difficult and a bit dangerous. At one point we could not steam forward among the rocks and collect our sample from the port side using the grab and winch, so Jim put the *Lady* in reverse and went in astern, with me on the transom directing us around the rocks. My deodorant wasn't working well then, but fortunately Jim and the *Lady* were. We managed, carefully and safely, to get all of our samples among the rocks and then maneuver around the island and continue to sample from the island to New Rochelle. I learned a good deal about water consciousness and water safety (and boat safety) by working with

R/V *Lady Barbara*. *Lady Barbara*'s afterdeck during a sampling cruise on the Sound in 1972. She looks more like a scientific research vessel here with the various sample buckets, cans, and bottles used to transport samples of fishes, bottom-living organisms, and Sound water back to the Ocean Science Lab on Montauk. All of that sampling equipment, plus the bottom trawl and gill net, made working on deck a bit hazardous at times. Working at sea, whether on a large oceanographic research vessel or a small day dragger, had to be done carefully and methodically to ensure safety, as well as the proper handling of samples. Jim Miller was a very cautious and careful seaman and demanded the same of anyone on *Lady Barbara*, where I always felt safe. There is a gull visitor resting on the *Lady*'s transom here. Gulls and other sea birds were common sights around fishing boats. It was common, also, for birds to land on board boats and rest for a time.

Jim. He knew his boat and the waters and took no chances that weren't understood and calculated.

Lady Barbara also was used as part of a study of the lobster population of Long Island Sound under a grant to the Ocean Science Lab from the New York State Department of Environmental Conservation (DEC). The DEC was studying the lobster population of the Sound and working with commercial lobstermen to obtain samples from their traps and pots. During the Lab's fisheries trawling studies in the western Sound aboard *Lady Barbara*, we frequently netted lobsters.

Most of them were "shorts," or biologically immature and legally undersized animals, that were too small to be caught in commercial lobster pots.

The pots were designed to retain the larger legal sized lobsters, while allowing the shorts to crawl out through the spaces between the pots' ribs. So, our trawl samples offered opportunities for the study of immature lobsters, and their distribution in the Sound, as a compliment to the DEC's study of larger mature lobsters. The study of immature and undersized marine animals suited me, as they were the future of the fishery, next year's harvest. We counted the lobsters captured by trawl, recorded their distribution in the Sound, and applied small tags to many of them for movement and migration studies. Periodic reports were provided to the DEC for their use in understanding and managing the Long Island Sound lobster fisheries. *Lady Barbara* proved to be a research vessel of many capabilities and many uses.

Jim Miller also proved his worth and was a constant source of enlightenment on the plight of Long Island's commercial fishermen. In the early 1970s, Jim was president of the Long Island Fishermen's Association. His brother Richard, a commercial lobsterman in Port Jefferson, was the Association's secretary. Jim and I had long discussions on fishery legislative matters and fishing in general while trawl sampling and especially during long travel times on the Sound between sampling points. Jim was concerned about fisheries and conservation regulations that seemed to be more restrictive on commercial fishermen than on recreational fishermen, who caught a lot of fish. Jim also was bothered by the seemingly never ending battles between recreational and commercial fishermen over access to beaches for fishing rights and privileges in what was viewed as common property. Jim was interested in what the East End baymen were doing and how they were approaching some of those legislative issues, which I could speak to. Those discussions helped to fuel my interest in the plight of local fishermen and the local fisheries.

On the Sound

We worked well together, Jim the seasoned captain and fishermen, and me the young biologist still learning. But, I got to instruct Jim, once, by showing him how to cook on *Lady Barbara*'s hot muffler, which he really liked. On one subsequent sampling venture, Jim took the lead as ship's steward and brought not only tin foil for the muffler, but lemon, butter, paper plates, and plastic knives and forks. I asked where were the tea cups and wine and we both smiled. Occasionally, I would take the *Lady*'s wheel for stretches of running time, and I even brought her into Port Jeff Harbor one night. Jim taught me the channel and the range lights used to guide incoming vessels to the dockage at the head of the Harbor during darkness. Bringing the *Lady* home at night using the Harbor range lights made me feel real salty, like a seasoned bayman. I liked Jim's teaching and mentoring, and I appreciated his confidence in me.

One of the Lab's employees who used to accompany me during sampling studies aboard *Lady Barbara* was Walt Job, a Montauk local. His father owned a hardware store in Montauk Village. Walt liked to work out-of-doors and onboard ship. Walt and Jim Miller got along famously and Walt was very helpful and steady during field work. He ran most of the Lab's smaller boats during the fisheries studies in East End waters and was a very careful waterman (much like Jim Miller) who contributed a lot to the team effort. Walt had an uncanny ability for staying dry while field sampling, even during the sloppiest of seas. I would be wet, cold, and miserable; Walt, dry and smiling.

Occasionally, he would have on hand a supplement to the field sampling and fishing gear, in the form of a small hip flask containing Southern Comfort. We just called it "Walt's hooch." He passed it around at the end of the day after sampling was completed, as we were packing up the gear before heading home. Being dry and warm, he didn't need it, but it felt good to this cold mariner. Walt did some bay scalloping on the side, usually in Lake Montauk, and he was reconstructing an old Jeep pickup to use as part of his new commercial fishing venture. He had the Jeep inside an old wooden frame hanger building on the Lab grounds. That old building dated back to when the Lab site property on Fort Pond Bay had been owned by the U.S. Navy. Walt worked on the Jeep during weekends. It was nearly complete and operational when a tremendous fire in 1974 completely destroyed the old building, and Walt's Jeep. And Walt, it sort of destroyed him as well. I recall him standing at the back door of the fisheries building, coffee cup in hand, staring silently at the charred and smoldering ruins of the hanger, the morning after the fire. No words were exchanged. The silence told of his lost efforts and shattered dream.

Leaky *Louise*

No recollection of working with and being mentored by experienced waterman and traditional baymen would be complete without a recounting of "Leaky *Louise*." In the mid-1970s, the Ocean Science Lab underwent some financial difficulties that made chartering *Lady Barbara* for extensive field work a bit too expensive. So, the Lab purchased its own small dragger, a 1920s vintage western rigged dragger, *Louise*. She was outfitted for trawling, with the help of Edwin Sherrill, Jr., an experienced and respected Amagansett bayman who advised the Lab and its fisheries staff on many commercial fishery matters. Ed told me that before World War II, *Louise*, then named *Netop*, was used as a charter fishing boat. During the War, the charter boat fishing business was reduced to zero. *Netop* then was converted to a commercial fishing dragger. She was part of the Montauk fleet then, but was purchased by the Lab from her owner in Shinnecock.

Ed was descended from some of East Hampton Town's earliest settlers. He was a terrific guy, very friendly, with an infectious smile and laugh. He owned an ocean dory he purchased from a builder in Nova Scotia. He moored it on Bonac Creek (Accabonac Harbor). I recall talking with Byron Young about Ed's dory. Byron insisted that the

Leaky *Louise.* The R/V *Louise* coming into dock at Port Jefferson Harbor in 1975. *Louise* was a 1920s vintage eastern-rigged dragger. She looks very similar to *Lady Barbara.* The difference in using *Louise* for marine research on Long Island Sound was the inexperienced crew running her, and her age. When we hung up the bottom trawl on an old wreck and nearly capsized *Louise*, it reinforced for me just how important experience and safety are at sea, and how hazardous commercial fishing can be. The man on the bow was Paul Broskus, one of the marine biologists from the Montauk Lab.

dory was not moored "in" Bonac Creek, but rather was "perched on" the Creek, because its draft was only a few inches of water. In fact, when viewed from the shore, Ed's dory did look to be perched on the water, seemingly without a draft at all. We laughed nicely about that, in full respect of both boat and owner. Ed spent more than 20 years working as a dragger fisherman, as crew for others, and on his own draggers.

He also shipped out many times as a volunteer crewman aboard R/V *Albatross IV* during the late 1970s through the mid-1990s. Ed was a public spirited man and very involved in issues of local importance and in local government. He was a professor and taught navigation and seamanship at Suffolk County Community College. Not long before I left the East End, Ed approached me about running for local office, Town Trustee, since the Trustees had jurisdiction over much of the estuarine bay bottomlands and thus over some local fishery resources. It seemed to me then that local government and the scientific or academic independence I felt, in being involved in local fisheries matters, might conflict, so I declined. I'm not sure to this day that I was correct about that or that I made the right decision. I am very sure, however, that I was honored and privileged at being asked to participate in local fisheries matters through local government service by respected people like Ed Sherrill.

Well, when *Louise* was purchased to be our local fishery sampling vessel, a skipper also was hired to pilot her. He had a Coast Guard license and had been a ferry captain at Fire Island and thus was an experienced mariner and boat operator. Unfortunately, however, he had no experience fishing or running a commercial dragger, and had no experience on Long Island Sound. We Lab fishery scientists were to fill that void. And a void it remained. All of my time at sea and my ship time aboard several vessels, even operating them occasionally, did not substitute for the knowledge and skill of an experienced bayman or waterman at the helm, someone who knew the work, the waters and the landscape of the bottom. The result was trawl net hang-ups on submerged wrecks and lost fishing gear, mechanical trouble at sea, and tows to port by the Eaton's Neck Coast Guard group. Data were lost, sampling was inconsistent, and frustrations ran high among the Lab staff.

I recall hanging up the bottom trawl on a wreck during fish sampling on the Sound in 1975 and our frustration at not being able to free it. We tried all manner of ways to pull the trawl free, unsuccessfully. Finally, we found ourselves directly above the snag trying to break free using *Louise*'s power winch. With all that effort to free the snagged trawl, I could see a dangerous situation unfolding. I went below to my duffel, found my wallet and put it in my pocket. I wanted some identification on my person in the event that I went overboard. One of the biologists was running the power winch while the skipper was in the wheelhouse (just the opposite of how we did it on *Lady Barbara*) and I was on the afterdeck watching and communicating what was happening. The winch was so strong that *Louise* began to list to one side and was on her way to overturning. I ran across the deck, lunged for the winch controls, and threw it out of gear. *Louise* then righted herself and bobbed for a few seconds. After that, we radioed the Coast Guard for assistance, and they did what we should have done by using a fire axe to cut the trawl cables and free *Louise*. That meant, of course, that we lost our fishing gear, and the day's sampling. And we had some things to explain when we returned to Montauk.

I grimace as I look back on all that ship time aboard *Kyma*, wallowing seasick in Block Island Sound, and green water washing o'er the decks of *Albatross* a hundred miles at sea, and then almost being pitched into a calm Long Island Sound by inexperienced hands on a 50 year old dragger. Those experiences with *Louise* after so much success with *Lady Barbara* were the source of much frustration. The floundering of *Louise* also must have foretold my fate, for within a few months of that adventure in 1975, I would be part of a reduction in staff at the Lab, itself starting to flounder. *Louise* eventually sank at dockside in Port Jeff Harbor, with only her radio antennae visible.

Catching and Sampling Live Animals

While working with the baymen, I used to get ribbed about always carrying a clipboard wherever I went, and for using the Lab's smaller "plastic" (fiberglass) boats, those ones that Walt Job was so good at operating. Real baymen had **wooden** boats after all. I used the clipboard and other field data books to record the sampling day's events, to record the scientific data, and to just remember what had happened, especially with all of those live animals and the ones we were bringing back to the Lab for study. To trust the mind to remember so many details was shaky, at best, and scientifically unsound. Recording data and observations at sea could be a real challenge, especially during foul weather and frigid winter work, especially for me, as I always seemed to be wet and cold.

On Long Island Sound, the best and the worst of weather could be found. Foul rainy weather did not bother me nearly so much, however, as hard wind and stormy seas, with the ever possibility of seasickness, which I experienced several times. But the baymen told me that even worse was snow. When there is a heavy snowfall at sea, the entire world is whited out and there is no sense of direction. Snow, even with calm seas and low wind, was very treacherous and very frightening, even more so than fog. Mariners adjust to fog, a common element in the lives of people who live by and on the sea. I recall Jimmy Lester's sixth water sense in the fog. But he didn't sail in snow. I appreciated very much being with experienced baymen and mariners who used common sense.

Those baymen who were proficient at their trade often did the very same note and record keeping that I did, or perhaps, I did what they did. At the end of their work day, having packed-out their harvest for shipment to market, many would record their day's catches by species and poundage in their own private log books. Some fishermen also made notes on other unusual fishes caught, on the weather conditions, on the places where they fished, and on the operation of their vessel. Those data provided them the information base they needed to keep track of their business and to improve their operations.

Those record books were guarded secrets. I was privileged to see such books now and then, in confidence, and was amazed at the accuracy and detail of the accounts of fishes and shellfishes harvested on a daily basis, along with information on young fishes released, odd species taken, and weather conditions. The private collection of those records among the many baymen and their families surely tell

Homeward Bound. A view of the sunset through *Kyma*'s port rail while steaming eastward on the Sound. Studying and sampling the marine environment often began before sunrise and finished after sunset. Sometimes, our field sampling was done to coincide with the tidal cycles, and at other times sampling was conducted in both daylight and darkness to learn about daily patterns of marine life. Sampling of the fishes for tagging and migration studies coincided with their seasonal availability. As such, we marine scientists often sampled in ways similar to the harvesting methods used by Long Island's commercial fishermen and the East End baymen who fished by the tides and with the seasons.

a marvelous story of the East End's fishes and the pursuit of them by generations of knowledgeable fishermen.

Scientific sampling, like commercial fishing, resulted in the compilation of information, data, and the keeping of records. During scientific field sampling operations, I had to ensure the accuracy and integrity of the collection of biological samples, the recording of data, and the assurance that the samples and information were taken properly while at sea and returned intact to the Lab. Data records and preserved specimens at sea had to be organized and indexed against date, time, place of collection, sampling gear type, and against related environmental information such as weather conditions, sea state, tidal stage, water temperature and salinity. If specimens and field records could not be cross-referenced back at the Lab, valuable information would be lost, making analyses difficult and written reports inaccurate. Science requires careful recording of information and observations both in the field and in the laboratory.

During inclement weather, field note taking and keeping became very difficult, making later interpretation in the laboratory difficult as well. I recall the story of a prominent oceanographer with the federal government who worked his way into an administrative position in Washington, D.C., after many years in various positions at several coastal laboratories. At one of the labs, he was responsible for computer storage and retrieval of the oceanographic data being collected by the field researchers. Some of the data received were in the form of field notes that had come from the vessels at sea during rough stormy weather. His transcribers and computer data handlers often complained of illegible notes, data, and hand writing, and of sloppy messy data sheets turned in from oceanographic field trips.

To remedy the situation, not only did the administrator encourage better care during field operations, he also methodically sent all of the office personnel to sea for a period of field sampling and data record keeping. Often, he would schedule their presence at sea when the weather forecasts called for inclement conditions. Needless to say, upon return to the office environment, complaints about sloppy field notes ceased to be a problem.

I took a phone call one day at the Lab from a commercial fisherman in Mattituck, on the northern shore of Eastern Long Island, who trawled for fishes regularly in Long Island Sound. Scup (or porgies) were especially plentiful there, seasonally, and an evening twilight tow close to shore could produce a nice net full for market. The fisherman had seen the results of some of our fisheries studies of the Sound and he was baffled why our tows there took so few fish, especially scup, when he knew from experience the Sound could be productive. Were we fishing improperly? Or concealing some information?

Our trawl net, I explained, was several times smaller (in mouth opening) than his, and we towed for a standard time of 15 minutes versus his commercial tows of up to an hour. And very often we had to sample during the day rather than at twilight. I explained, also, that our net was of a standard size used in scientific studies and that it was important to be consistent with sampling gear and methods, so that data from different areas and different years could be compared and contrasted. I recall feeling that my best efforts at explaining fell on deaf ears. But I tried. And I knew that fishermen were concerned about their waters and their livelihood, and they tried to understand we scientists and our work, especially when it might affect them and their livelihood. And I have long admired the East End fishing communities for trying amid great pressures to hold to traditions and maintain the life styles passed down from centuries during which my forefathers were still in Europe.

Live Animals and Ethical Challenges

Some of our studies of the Sound's fishes required the use of a beach seine to sample the shore zone and the fishes that might be close to, or influenced by, human activities, such as LILCO's Northport power station on the Sound. When we studied the fishes at Northport, we used a seine net that was 800 feet long and resembled a small commercial haul seine. It was set by boat from the beach near the power station, much like the baymen did in the ocean on the East End. We then retrieved the net by hand, with two people hauling on each end, much as had been done by the baymen before trucks and power winches came into use in the 1950s or so. At the end of a winter's day of hauling that seine at several sites near Northport, I was exhausted. Walt's hooch helped.

I recall one particular day of seining for fishes near the Northport power station when we took a small school of striped mullet (*Mugil cephalus*) a pretty shimmering fish filled with energy and speed. As we were about to haul in the bunt, several of the mullet swam around in circles, at the surface, within the entrapment of the net. At one point they swam straight toward where we were standing on the beach holding the net, then they turned abruptly and quickly swam straight offshore and leaped over the float line, just as pretty as you please, shimmering silvery white in the sun. Never having seen striped mullet before, I stood motionless watching. I could not help but smile with awe and respect. Striped mullet are visitors to Long Island waters, being natives and spawners in more southern waters of the East Coast. There they are called "jumping mullet" or simply "jumpers," as they are known to escape capture in commercial nets by doing just what I observed. We did catch several of their cohorts at Northport that day, however, and I recall some displeasure at having to preserve in formalin (for examination later) such beautiful and spirited animals.

Thinking back on field sampling, and especially with those baymen, watermen, and mariners with whom I was privileged to work, brought to mind my earliest attempts to be a conscientious and ethical field biologist when catching, sampling, and studying live fishes. My ethics in those matters would be enhanced and refined by working beside Jimmy Lester at his pound nets in Fort Pond Bay, and with Jim Miller while dragging Long Island Sound aboard *Lady Barbara*.

My first real scientific experience studying live fishes came when I was conducting the field and lab research for my masters thesis at Long Island University. In the summer and fall of 1970, I collected live cunners for my research on the blood physiology, or hematology, of wild and captive fish. I studied the hematology of fish called "cunners" or "bergalls" (scientifically, one of those long Latin names, *Tautogolabrus adspersus*). Cunners are abundant year-round species in the northeast inshore marine and estuarine waters and are easily captured by a variety of methods. They can be caught and returned alive many times without any visible stress, which I learned as a sport

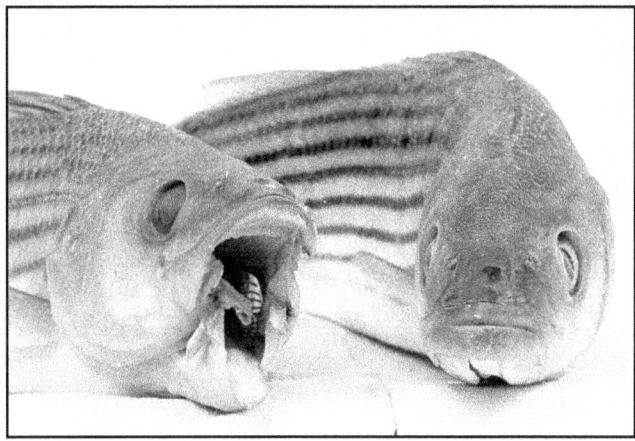

Injured Striped Bass. The fish on the left is an injured striped bass we caught by haul seine at Northport, on Long Island Sound in 1972. The striped bass on the right is normal and uninjured. The injured bass was a 10-inch long, three-year-old female fish with no lower jaw. It was smaller in length and weight than two-year old bass taken in the same area. The injury had stunted its growth, presumably due to reduced feeding ability. Amazingly, however, it was still alive a year after the injury appeared to have taken place. The hardiness of that fish attracted my attention and I continued to observe injured and abnormal fish (especially striped bass) during the Montauk Lab's fishery research projects. *Photo by Carl Mamay.*

fisherman. I caught my cunners for research from Oyster Bay on Long Island's north shore. Oyster Bay connects to Long Island Sound's central basin.

My thesis studied the hematology of cunners caught in the wild and then held in captivity in the lab in order to compare the results and understand their ability to tolerate the stress of captivity. Cunners often are found in water under the influence of human activities, thus understanding their ability to tolerate stress might help understand their ability to tolerate pollution. For the field testing, I devised a method of capturing them, quickly anesthetizing them, drawing a small amount of blood with a needle and syringe, and then placing them into a recovery tank. The entire procedure took 2–4 minutes. I used this blood drawing process for fish caught in the wild and for

On the East End

fish in the lab. On board ship, I held the fish for 6–8 hours in a recovery tank continuing bay water. Those fish allowed to recover in the lab generally were held overnight. I released all of the fish back in the estuarine environment some distance away from the capture site. The distance factor was to guard against recapturing the same fish again and possibly skewing my data.

Once I had refined the blood drawing and handling procedures, 95% of my captured and tested cunners survived. I then could release the fish back into the bay environment with some confidence that they would survive. After completing one part of my study, I took a group of cunners from a lab recovery tank at the University to Great South Bay on Long Island's south shore to release them. I transported them in one of those state-of-the-art fish transportation containers that graduate students can afford, a large plastic trash can with a portable battery powered air pump and airstone. I carried the plastic can from my car to the Bay, stepped into the water about knee deep and gently lowered the can into the water so that the cunners could swim out. As they swam out, they all turned around and huddled together around my legs and ankles. It made me feel really good, all warm and fuzzy, like they trusted me and were saying goodbye. Of course what they really were doing was swimming to the nearest object for safety. Guess my legs looked like pilings. But I was pleased at being able to study the fish and then release them alive back into their environment.

Several years later, in 1982, I published a portion of my thesis in a respected national scientific journal, the *Transactions of the American Fisheries Society*. During the journal's review process of my manuscript, the journal editor wrote me that he had been advised to remove the discussion on my techniques for recovery of the cunners and their 95% survival rate. Apparently the reviewers felt that it was not relevant to my methods and scientific findings. I was dismayed at this suggestion and the thought that the journal reviewers did not

On the Sound

First, Do No Harm. These fishes were my friends. They are cunners, also called bergalls, in a recovery tank following their use for physiological health studies. Cunners are hardy animals that live in inshore or near shore waters and feed around docks, pilings, wharfs, and jetties. During my master's thesis research, I caught them by hook and line in Oyster Bay, NY. After conducting blood tests on them, I was able to return them alive to another Long Island embayment. A few years later, cunners were part of the fish catch in bottom-trawl samples on Long Island Sound during an ecological study I participated in. Sometimes the trawl samples produced large numbers of fishes that needed to be identified, sorted, counted, sampled, preserved, or returned to sea. I tried to preserve live fish samples quickly so that the fishes would not lie on deck and suffer while awaiting their ultimate fate.

seem concerned about my ethical treatment and the survival of experimental fishes. I felt that it was important to demonstrate that cunners could be captured, handled, and survive experimentation. I also liked the ethics of returning alive the fish I captured and studied, and I wanted that in print. So, I explained and politely objected to the reviewers' advice and requested that the full discussion be retained in the published paper. The editor agreed and the discussion was retained.

In that research, I tried to follow an ethic of "first doing no harm." I had sacrificed a few cunners during the initial phases of the experimental testing, but I had endeavored to do better. I'm sure that the northeast population of cunner did not suffer from the few I had killed, and the several that I released alive probably did not sustain the population either. I was pleased to have made a successful effort at personally doing minimal harm, however, and providing advice to others in my paper on how to do the same. I had stuck with my personal ethics.

The practice and principle of releasing fishes to the environment would change a bit for me, however, in the years to follow, and my ethics of involvement with live fishes would be challenged and tested, especially on the Sound. As I've discussed, I participated in the field studies and sampling of the fish populations all around Long Island, using many methods, including bottom trawl, beach seine, mid-water trawl, gill net, plankton net, and even by monitoring the fishes impinged on the cooling water intake screens of the Northport power plant. I also worked with local baymen and observed the fishes caught in their trawls, pound nets, and beach haul seines. I am sure that I participated in the capture and sampling of, literally, hundreds-of-thousands, and probably even millions of fishes.

Many fishes I counted and identified while they still were in the nets, some were tagged, and then returned alive. I could not even begin to estimate how many fish I removed for study. Those fishes kept for study later were caught by net, removed from the water, and packaged for eventual transport back to a laboratory for analysis, and for use as reference samples. At times, a good portion of the fish taken in those field samples were not needed for later study, died on deck, and sometimes were returned to the water dead. There was a time toward the end of my tenure at the Montauk Lab during which I handled so many fish of every description and condition (alive, dead, iced, frozen, rotting, injured, diseased, preserved in formalin or alcohol) that I lost my appetite for fish. It took a couple of years away from that work to fully regain my taste for good fresh fish. I cannot now eat fish (or any seafood, for that matter), without recalling this.

My idealism and old-fashioned sympathy were enlivened on the Sound, and I began to feel badly about catching and killing so many fishes for study. So, I tried to do a better job of keeping the netted fish in water while they were being sorted, counted and sampled, so that they could be returned alive. I also tried to be more efficient at figuring out, beforehand, what portion of a netted catch would be needed for later study, so as not to take back to the Lab more than were actually needed for analysis. I consulted a biological statistician for help in sample design.

I began to feel a bit guilty about all those fishes we caught by trawl that were being counted and sorted while they were suffocating to death on the deck of *Lady Barbara*, or in our 800 foot seine net on the beach. So, I tried being "kinder" to those fishes that would be taken back to the Lab. I thought that perhaps a quicker death than suffocation on the deck of the boat would be better and more humane for those fish that were needed for later study. On one sampling trip aboard the *Lady*, I took several jugs of a pre-mixed preservative called formalin (a solution of 10% formaldehyde) into which I would place the fish immediately upon capture, thinking that this would be an easier death for them than suffocating on deck while I sorted and counted the catch.

With the first retrieval of the bottom trawl, I placed a few fishes into one of the jugs, thinking that I was being more humane than in the past. One of the first fish that went into the jug was a cunner, the species that I had studied for my master's thesis, and a species I had come to admire for its hardiness and resourcefulness, the species I had taken pains to return alive to the bay after studying it in the lab. Upon being put into the jug of formalin, the cunner swam furiously and nervously from side to side, crashing into the glass of the jug. It bumped its snout against the glass and beat its body furiously as if to try to push its way out through the glass, all the while facing me and looking straight at me. I swear, it looked as if it was trying to tell me that I had not done the humane thing there. After several minutes, it went belly up and died. I felt as though I had tortured it.

That night at home, I had a dream, a nightmare actually, that I was caught by some fishes and thrown into a jug of formalin to be tortured to death. True story. I still remember that dream and still can see that cunner, facing me in the jug and giving me its body language that I had done ill by it. To this day, more than 35 years later, I still feel that way, and I shiver as I remember it. But, I did receive that cunner's message! I didn't use the formalin approach again in the field and I tried to be a responsible sampler of live fishes, taking only what was needed and returning alive as many as possible.

I have a few special 35mm color slides in my collection that I use during talks and seminars on fisheries and conservation, especially in public school science classes. One such slide shows several cunners in a fish tank, those fishes I studied for my masters and then released alive. There is another slide that is a close up of a small live killifish or mummichog (*Fundulus* sp.) looking through the glass of a laboratory fish tank in which I housed it, many years ago. It is looking at me head-on, much as did that cunner in the formalin jug.

When I would enter the laboratory in the morning and flick on the lights, that killifish would look at me head-on and follow my movements all around the lab. I always wondered what it might have been thinking, if it could do so. Perhaps it was wondering what sort of experiment it would be subjected to each day. I returned it to the bay. The title of the 35mm slide, I hand wrote on its border, is "who's watching who?" I learned a great deal from that killifish and those cunner. I pass on that learning to students and other fishery scientists as a charge, whenever possible, to first do no harm, be careful, and avoid undesirable or unintended consequences from their work. I've shared those ethical experiences with my fisheries colleagues

Execution Rocks Light. Execution Rocks Light is on a small island located in the extreme western basin of Long Island Sound. While conducting a study of bottom-living organisms aboard the dragger *Lady Barbara* in 1972 I photographed the Coast Guard lighthouse there. The tidal range in the western Sound could reach as much as 8–9 feet; the range in the eastern Sound was much less. I have always liked lighthouses and admired their mission on behalf of mariners at sea. Seek a lighthouse and you likely will find a local museum, local history, and perhaps a good seafood restaurant nearby.

through newsletters of professional associations such as the American Institute of Fishery Research Biologists and the National Association of Academies of Science.

When I worked for the federal government in the late 1970s, I helped to prepare an environmental impact statement on the effects of an electric generating station, a power plant, on fishes and fisheries in the river on which the plant was located. I participated in the public hearing that examined the impact statement and I testified as an expert witness on the fisheries aspects of the impact assessment. In order to understand the possible effects of the power plant on the river fishes, the utility company conducted netting studies that sampled the river fish populations. I testified at the hearing that the company's river netting studies captured more fishes than were estimated to have been affected by the operation of the power plant. I suggested that the power company should reevaluate and redesign the river studies to capture fewer live fishes. I saw similar occurrences at other power plant sites and wrote about some of them in an effort to draw attention to the matter. My time with fishermen on the Sound, on Fort Pond Bay, on the East End beaches educated me on environmental ethics that should matter to scientists.

Jim Miller watched me struggling with those trawl catches and the live fishes onboard *Lady Barbara* and I told him of my nightmare with the cunners. He was very tolerant of this itinerant and slightly eccentric field biologist. When I fished with Jimmy Lester, the ability to cull out the keeper fishes and to return alive all the rest really appealed to me. Jimmy was a really good sport in tolerating my whims in that regard, also, especially when I nurtured one of his old his nemeses, that dogfish shark, and helped it birth several live pups.

!@#$%&* scien'ists is right, Cap! I shared many of these sea stories and sampling adventures with Jimmy as we tended his traps, trawled aboard *Tern*, and just talked at home. I also shared many of them with the baymen during their monthly Association business meetings at the Town Marine Museum. My misadventures on the water usually brought a smile and a laugh. And I smile every time I recall those wonderful people and those wonderful years on Long Island, and especially on the East End.

5

The Last Best Times?

These pages recall the Long Island fishing community where I lived and with whom I worked and learned. They try not to paint an overly rosy picture of the East End fishing community in the 1970s, but they may be painting the end of an era. I have tried to recount the people and the times as I remember them. Time, however, can take a toll on the memory, and it tends to retain the good and positive things and discard much of the rest. I have been told by some East Enders that the early 1970s were among the best times there. I cannot quantify or verify that from their points of view. Peter Matthiessen's accounts of the fishing community in his 1986 book *Men's Lives*, as well as the recent environmental accounts of the East End's marine resources prepared by the Peconic Estuary Program in 1991 and the Peconic Baykeeper in 2006, all suggest that the 1970s were relatively productive and healthy years environmentally. In looking back and remembering the East End's environment and its fishing community as I knew them then, those years seem as robust and vigorous ones. I hope they were not the last best times.

Vigor of the Fishing Community

In the 1970s, the vigor of the local fishing community was expressed or manifested by many fisherman in pursuit of a variety and diversity of finfish and shellfish resources. The local and regional stocks of important fishery species were abundant and supported the vigor of the fishing community and fueled its spirit. Important finfish and shellfish harvests peaked then. The baymen fished using traditional methods. Families of fishermen, often several generations of people, worked together as they practiced their craft. Young fishers, male and female, worked beside and learned from their elders. The fishers were very competitive in their work of fishing, but they would aid each other when needed in the work and in their community lives. The East Hampton Town Baymen's Association was very active in local and regional political matters that affected them and the marine environment on which they relied.

The Baymen's Association worked with the Long Island Fishermen's Association on important industry matters. Membership was extended to non-fishermen who supported the Baymen's Association's goals and purpose. Several of the fishermen and the fishing crews assisted the DEC and the Ocean Science Lab on Montauk with scientific conservation studies on important fishery species, especially striped bass. Some fishermen would contact local scientists when unusual or rare fish species were caught. The Baymen's Association hosted an annual clam chowder dinner open to the public. The

The Last Best Times?

A Cooperative Effort. This is the side panel from a waxed box used to pack and ship fresh fish from the East End into New York City's Fulton Fish Market. Many fishermen in the East Hampton Town Baymen's Association worked collaboratively to create the East Hampton Town Sea Food Producers Cooperative, Inc., chartered in 1974. The "Co-op" was a wholesale and retail enterprise where the fishermen could bring their daily harvests for shipping into the City and/or for sale in the local community. The fishermen also could share in the cost of icing, boxing, and shipping the fish, as well as purchase equipment at less cost through the Co-op.

Sharing in the Co-op. In 1974, stock was offered for sale in the new East Hampton Town Sea Food Producers Cooperative, Inc. While I was a card-carrying member of the Baymen's Association, I was not a "producer" — a commercial fisherman. I never earned a nickel from my fishing or working with the baymen, but occasionally I would receive a nice fish to take home for dinner at the end of the fishing day. What I did gain was learning for a lifetime. Give me a fish and you feed me for a day; teach me to fish and you feed me for a lifetime.

On the East End

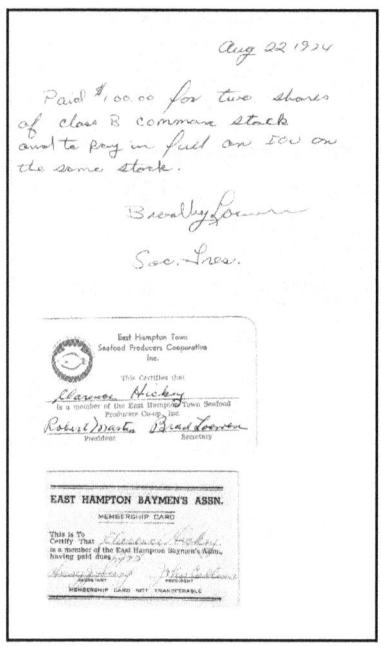

Card Carrying Member. The formality and informality of the fishing community are shown by my membership cards in the Co-op and the Baymen's Association, and by my receipt for two shares of Class B stock in the Co-op. Such was my status in the fishing community, formally a member of the Baymen's Association as one interested in what it stood for, but not a fisherman or seafood "producer." I treasure those roles and these documents. During the early planning and development stages of the Co-op, its new corporate leaders (all baymen) took me to lunch and offered me the job of Co-op manager. What a thrill and an honor that was, but I declined the offer and remained in my scientific and marine biology job. But I have often looked back and wondered, "What if ... ."

Association also created a Sea Food Producers Cooperative to assist the fishermen with their businesses. It contained a sea food market open to the public. The Sea Food Co-op was relatively short lived, but it was born out of a need and a community concern. The women in the fishing community often participated in the fishing, managed their husband's fishing business, and ran and managed important supporting functions, such as the Baymen's Association Ladies Auxiliary and the *Baymen's Association Newsletter*. The local commercial fishing community also had an advocate or champion in Perry B. Duryea, Jr., who was Speaker of the New York State Assembly during the late 1960s and early 1970s. Mr. Duryea lived on Montauk and operated a family wholesale seafood business there. He had worked with his father as a commercial lobsterman. In the Legislature, Mr. Duryea was an influential voice in speaking on behalf of the commercial fishing community. In 1978, Mr. Duryea ran for Governor of New York and lost, and then left public life, returning to

The Last Best Times?

Seafood for Sale. I recall the busyness of the Co-op's retail seafood shop during the summer, and especially on the weekends. Here, seafood in the iced counter at the Co-op is being examined by a customer in 1975. He may have been in the market to buy some fish, but what he really did, however, was what author Peter Matthiessen — quoting Sir Walter Scott — described: "It's not fish ye're buyin, it's men's lives." — men's lives and the fishing tradition of the East End. My wife Mary worked at the Co-op in 1975 doing all manner of jobs behind the retail counter and behind the scenes in the kitchen.

the family seafood business on Montauk. The local fishing community has not had such an influential public figure speaking for it since.

That vigor of the fishing community appears to have been changing since about the mid-1980s. Baymen now advise their children to find work other than fishing, on the land, where the work is more steady. When the salty old baymen pass on, there are few to pick up the mantle of leadership and mentorship. Some fishing families have moved off of the East End, some have gone south. The environment no longer supports a natural resource base with the diversity and abundance that once sustained a robust community of fishermen and fishing families, and gave them and their East End community a cultural identity. This has made it hard for fishing families to make a living and to afford to live on the East End, where wealthy people from afar are making their homes (or second homes) and driving up the cost of living.

A rebuilt and once again robust East Coast striped bass population, however, has revitalized that coastal fishery, even though the relatively unrestricted fishing of previous times is a thing of the past. Harvest is permitted by the recreational and commercial fisheries, but in a very limited way that is strictly regulated and monitored. A segment of the East End's traditional fishing community, however, has been kept out of the vigor and vitality of the revitalized striped bass resource. In 1985, the mid-Atlantic coastal fishery for striped bass was legally closed. It was reopened in 1990, however, the New York State DEC stopped all ocean beach haul seining in New York State that same year. It has not been allowed yet to resume. Commercial fishing for striped was permitted by means other than haul seine at a restricted level that was monitored by the State.

Many of those haul seine fishermen had assisted the DEC with their conservation studies in the 1970s, some of the very studies that were used by the coastal states in their collective decision to close and rebuild the striped bass fisheries beginning in 1985. When those fisheries were reopened five years later, after the striped bass population revived, haul seine fishing in New York still was not permitted. Those fishermen who assisted in the conservation studies and who sacrificed during the five-year fishery closure, could not participate in the revitalized fishery using the traditional haul seine methods. Those who assisted and sacrificed, thusly, have not been part of the success that has been realized. They should be. People who undergo personal sacrifice for environmental enhancement, revitalization, or protection should be able to participate in reaping some of the environmental rewards, be they clean breathable air, clean water, healthy forests, or a piece of the harvest of vital fish stocks. Sacrifice should lead to reward when the environmental programs are successful.

Fisheries management efforts need to include the fishing community along with the biological fish stocks. Fishers and fishes need to be nurtured and sustained. Both need to be valued and made as whole as possible. Both need to be part of environmental management systems. This was the concept described by Professor Svein Jentoft in a 1999 article in the American Fisheries Society journal

The Last Best Times?

Rebuilding Fish Stocks and the Human Community. There were several haul seine crews with whom we worked during the DEC's and the Montauk Lab's striped-bass studies in the early 1970s. This truck and dory were part of bayman Dominic Grace's crew. Other crews I recall then were led by baymen Danny King, Pete Kromer, and William Havens. The Lesters had at least one crew, led by Calvin Lester, and may have had another led by Francis and Jens Lester. All these crews were from East Hampton town. There were a few additional crews, also, that came from Southampton town to the west.

Many of those baymen cooperated, to some degree, in the striped bass conservation studies. The State of New York curtailed haul seine fishing in 1990 as part of the effort to rebuild the fish stock. This traditional way of fishing has not been allowed to resume. (Striped bass may now be harvested commercially by other means, but not by haul seining.) If the coastal striped bass stock maintains its rebuilt vigor and is sustainable, some level of haul seine harvest ought to be considered. A low level of legal harvest by haul seining would breath new life into the East End community and provide evidence that sacrifice for conservation can result in future rewards.

Environmental regulations need to consider people while the environmental resources are being restored,. The traditional fishers and their community have paid a price for conservation. While we care for the fishes, the fishers also need to be nurtured. Environmental laws need to steward both the people and the environment.

Fisheries. Jentoft explained that fisheries management should not damage the social structure and culture of fishing communities. He stated: "government-initiated regulatory systems are eroding community solidarity and cohesiveness ... fisheries management must consist of more than just rules and regulations that curb fishing effort. Management must include strategies of community development, including the building of a civic society.... Before we can even hope to rebuild stocks, we must start to rebuild communities."

In order to reward those who participated and sacrificed in the conservation efforts, and to prop up a segment of the social fishing culture of the East End, the State of New York could revisit the decision to ban haul seining on the East End's ocean beaches, especially for striped bass. Apparently, there was an attempt to allow a very limited haul seine fishery in the 1990s, for fish other than striped bass, but it was rejected by the commercial fishing community as too restrictive. The relatively unrestricted haul seine harvests of striped bass prior to the 1980s are a thing of the past. A renewed haul seine harvest that is limited in scope, strictly regulated, and monitored might be able to rejoin the coastal fishery once again.

I understand that such a limited fishery may not be economically viable. In regaining this old traditional fishing method, however, even in a limited way, the East End would regain a piece of itself and a connection to its past. In this way, a fishery management system that includes and values fishers, as well as the fishes, could contribute to building, and hopefully sustaining, a coastal human community. Wholeness among the people will lead to more integrity and wholeness of the environment that sustains them. This dysfunctional fishery and its management system are another sign or symptom of the collapsing vigor and the condition of the East End marine resources and the people linked with them. The last best times seem to be behind all of us and we all should be concerned about this.

Vigor of the Local Scientific Community

Another aspect of local fisheries conservation that needs to be revitalized is some form of open professional communication among the local scientific conservation community and the public. During the 1980s when the brown tide algae bloom appeared, and the striped bass and bay scallop resources were collapsing, the State of New York discontinued publication of its *New York Fish and Game Journal* for budget and financial reasons. That action, in 1986, resulted in removing an important communications tool among conservation scientists and between the scientists and the public. I was really bummed out by that decision. The *Fish and Game Journal* was a wonderful mechanism for local researchers and conservation managers to publish current natural resources information, especially research sponsored or conducted by the DEC. Fishery biologists I knew in New Jersey liked the *Journal* and lamented that the State of New Jersey did not have such a conservation publication for locally focused research.

The last issue of the *Journal*, dated July 1986, contains a nice research article by DEC biologist Byron Young and colleagues on the sport fisheries, including striped bass, at Montauk during 1973–1975. In the mid-1980s, important East End shell fishery resources were dwindling due to pollution and a brown tide algae bloom. At the same time, some coastal finfishery conservation management systems, such as for striped bass, were in need of attention. Consequently, the baymen and the commercial fishing community were adversely affected, while the State was cutting back on a valuable and useful conservation communication vehicle in the *Fish and Game Journal*. The mid-1980s seems to have been a rough time for Long Island's marine resources, those people studying them, and those people dependent on them for a livelihood.

Some natural resources, conservation, and environmental management studies and reports that are important locally, or perhaps regionally, are of lesser interest to a national scientific audience. Such studies thus often are not appropriate for publication in more widely read national scientific journals and magazines. They are appropriate for local audiences, scientific and public, and that's where local conservation publications like the *Fish and Game Journal* play an important role. The *Fish and Game Journal* and its contents, however, did have a fairly wide distribution. That was partly accomplished through some of the journal abstracting services that kept tabs on the current issues of many scientific and conservation journals and magazines and published their tables of contents.

Two of those abstracting services that published abstracts of my *Journal* papers were *Aquatic Sciences & Fisheries Abstracts* published by the Food and Agricultural Organization of the United Nations, and *Fish Health Abstracts* published by the U.S. Fish and Wildlife Service. As a result, I received hundreds of communications, literally, from across the USA and around the world from scientists requesting copies of papers I authored in the *Fish and Game Journal*. The paper Jimmy Lester and I published in the *Journal* in 1983 on "The Fishes of Fort Pond Bay on Long Island, New York" brought requests for copies from New York State (of course), and from Louisiana, Maryland, Massachusetts, North Carolina, Oklahoma, Pennsylvania, and from Canada. Our 1976 paper on "Tarpon from Montauk, New York" was requested by a professor from the University of Messina in Italy, as was the 1976 paper Brad Loewen and I wrote on "New Record for the Greater Amberjack from New York Waters." Several, of the other papers I authored in the *Journal* brought communications and requests for copies from most of the U.S. states, and from 26 foreign countries on both sides of the equator and the international date line.

In the last issue of the *Journal* in 1986, the editorial staff stated that "The agency [the DEC] reserves the right to continue publication at a future date." I believe that date has come. The East End environment and its fishing community continue to deteriorate and are in need of renewed investment from all corners of society—personal, public, corporate, and governmental. Conservation and environmental scientists and managers need to communicate openly with each other and the public. A good local and regional conservation journal could help to enable this, as it did in the past. The opportunity to publish in such a journal would reward local conservation scientists and managers for hard work in the public interest. Publishing in the former *Fish and Game Journal* always felt like a reward, and a privilege, to me.

Of course, it will take more than striped bass, ocean haul seining, and a renewed *Fish and Game Journal* to ensure the vitality of the East End's environment, its natural resources, and its cultural identity. It will take an extended and whole community.

"Man-to-Man" Must Come First

Conservationist Aldo Leopold wrote an essay entitled "The Ecological Conscience" in 1949 in which he argued that people need to change their behavior and conduct toward the land (i.e., the environment) in order to keep the environment in proper working order. In the essay, Leopold contrasted his view on peoples' relation to each other with people's relation to the land environment. He wrote:

"I have no illusion about the speed or accuracy with which an ecological conscience can become functional. It has required 19 centuries to define decent man-to-man conduct and the process is only half done; it may take as long to evolve a code of decency for man-to-land conduct."

I have come to believe that "decent man-to-land conduct," or human environmental stewardship and Earth healing, will not be possible on a societal scale until humanity is whole and in a right relationship, in a "decent man-to-man" or a "community" relationship.

Earth healing and stewardship begin with people healing. They come from people valuing each other and working together on common issues of survival and quality of life. This includes the people who use resources, the people who regulate resource use, and the people who are passionate about protecting resources. If people value each other, they will work cooperatively to value those aspects of the natural world they hold in common, the environment and the resources that sustain them. A whole and well people are better equipped and better able to focus on making, together, a whole, sustainable, East End natural environment. A renewed and sustainable East End environment would have regional implications.

Sustainability of the East End's environment is as much of a moral dilemma as a scientific or technical one. The East End's environment and natural resources need to be nurtured and stewarded by **all** who have an interest in or a stake in them. This includes all people who use, take from, or put back into the environment. It includes the native and resident people, as well as all those who visit the East End seasonally and use its lands, waters, beaches, and bays. Those with second homes who live on the East End or rent their homes there are among the stakeholders. Those who come from New York counties to the west and north to fish or boat on the East End are stakeholders, as are those from nearby states who vacation on the East End and arrive by car, train, airplane, ferry, or private boat.

All those who do business on or with the East End, whether the business is actually located there or whether it is located elsewhere and buys or sells with the East End from afar, these too are stakeholders. The well being of the East End's environment, and the vigor and robustness of its natural resources, are dependent on all of these stakeholders doing their part to honor each other and be "in community" with each other. It is dependent on all of these stakeholders honoring the environmental and conservation laws, but also exercising a community-focused environmental ethic that stewards the resources common to all. Exploitation of the natural resources and the naturalness of the East End are degrading the qualities that have brought and still bring people there. All of the stakeholders need to rise up and work collectively for the common good, before the natural values that attracted them to the area become too degraded and no longer attractive.

Everyone needs to think and act beyond themselves for the common good. Good local advice in this regard is contained in the Peconic Estuary Program's *Comprehensive Conservation and Management Plan* that was approved in 2001. This *Plan* reiterates repeatedly that all East End stakeholders (the residents, visitors, and businesses) need to participate in nurturing the watershed, estuarine, and marine environments. Similarly, the Peconic Baykeeper's first bay health report issued in 2006 also offers sound advice on community focused efforts and the building of a **collective** environmental ethic.

An aspect of this collective environmental ethic should include what would appear to be a general environmental stewardship principle: that those who participate in and sacrifice for environmental healing and wholeness should participate in reaping of the environmental rewards, when restoration is achieved. This principle needs to be held up and propped up as the East End works toward environmental wholeness and restoration of the Peconic/Gardiner's Bay system. All of the populace, citizenry, and stakeholders need to know and understand that if they participate and sacrifice for the environmental common good in supporting the Peconic Estuary Program and the Peconic Baykeeper efforts, they will be able to participate in reaping a portion of the benefits of a renewed and restored Bay system. The agencies involved in these efforts should not let the example of the haul seiners being excluded from the restored striped bass fishery serve as an example of the opposite.

On the East End

Respect for the Environment. The author examining a great white shark. In the summer of 1974, a year before the movie *Jaws* was released, this great white shark was caught in the Atlantic Ocean off Montauk. It was reported to have been 16 feet long and weighing 4,000 pounds. A father and son, fishing aboard a small cabin cruiser, hooked the shark and fought it to its death. It was towed into Montauk Harbor and placed on the docks for all to see. The New York Ocean Science Laboratory was called and asked to send a scientist to the docks to examine the shark. By the time I arrived on the scene, a crowd of people had gathered and the shark had been cut open by people wanting to know what it had eaten. People were leaning on it and poking it, just wanting to touch it. It was a form of public humiliation for such a great animal.

I refused to see *Jaws* in the theater in 1975 because the movie seemed to further the misunderstanding of sharks and the continued slaughter of them. Great whites and other such large fishes are the top predators of the marine environment. When top predators are hunted without regard for the numbers taken, their reduced abundance can have profound effects on the entire ecosystem.

It is now generally believed that the great white shark population is a threatened species in the Northwest Atlantic. Conservation laws now regulate the taking of most of the large migratory shark species. Many recreational shark fishermen now practice catch-and-release fishing. This kind of fishing exercises ethical behavior that goes far beyond the minimum environmental requirements of the conservation laws.

Community Among Resource Users

Professor James Acheson, of the University of Maine Department of Anthropology, wrote about the research he had conducted on the coastal lobster fisheries in the State of Maine. One of his scientific articles discussed the connection between the human communities of fishers, their unwritten codes of fishing behavior, and the effects that behavior had on the coastal lobster stocks on which the fishers depended. It related how some of the commercial fishing communities on the coast of central Maine had achieved economic stability, as well as sustainable local stocks of lobsters, by the voluntary conservation measures they imposed on themselves. Those measures resulted from the local mores that informally governed the fishing behavior of the lobstermen, behavior such as voluntarily limiting the numbers of lobster traps used by the fishermen and an agreed-upon local closed fishing season during which the lobsters were molting.

Those local unwritten, non-legally-binding, conservation measures did more than the State of Maine's formal conservation laws and regulations to conserve the local lobster stocks in some areas, compared with lobsterman in other Maine communities who just adhered to the formal State conservation laws only. The unwritten voluntary measures worked because everyone fishing in those local areas worked for the common good and adhered to the local mores, as well as to the formal state laws. Those lobstermen also felt a "sense of ownership" of the lobster resources in their areas and a responsibility for them. Their voluntary behavior and conservation actions had beneficial outcomes on both the environment and the quality of their own lives. Their actions demonstrated how conservation, and indeed environmental protection, depends on more than just obeying the legally enacted laws of society.

Sometimes it appears that legally binding conservation and environmental rules and regulations let some people off the hook when it comes to their personal environmental ethics. They believe that if they just obey the laws, everything will be OK. After all, that's what the laws are for, right? Well, not quite. For some, the laws means that they don't have to do any more than just obey the laws. They don't have to exercise any choice or personal ethics in their interaction with the environment, its living resources, or the other people who use and depend on the resources. I have found that environmental rules and regulations really are the minimum, the base, of what is needed to really protect the environment on behalf of the common good. Those Maine lobstermen actually were modeling for the rest of us what needs to be done to protect our resources and our environment, for both their proper use today and for their longer term sustainability. Their lobstering communities counted more on each other than on just the central authority of the conservation laws to protect the resources important to them. The people of those lobster fishing communities valued each other and their environment. Their cooperative behavior actually affected positively the quality of their resources and thus the quality of their own lives. Healthy fishery resources require healthy fishing communities.

In a similar way, we East End stakeholders should not let the conservation laws or the government regulatory agencies replace us in protecting and stewarding our environment by just the rule of law. The local government should assist, support, advise, guide, coach, and teach us, but never replace us as environmentally conscious citizens. Conservations laws tend to place the responsibility for environmental protection with government, rather than with the people where it belongs.

Cooperative behavior among the citizenry may be a form of altruism, a behavior that promotes the survival and well being of the human group or community at the expense of the individuals within the community. The altruistic behavior, of adhering to the unwritten local conservation mores, may have motivated cooperation and promoted harmony within the lobster fishing community, and eliminated or prevented conflict. The cooperative and altruistic behavior strengthened the bonds between and among the fishers and resulted in community solidarity. Those lobstermen who behaved selflessly and sacrificed for the community helped the community to do well and contributed to a healthy environmental commons in the form of a sustainable lobster population.

Unfortunately, The East End citizenry may not have such control over a single species fishery as did those Maine lobstermen. The East End fishing community depends on multiple species. And the baymen depend on being flexible, fishing with the seasons and with the diversity of species, some species that are resident in East End waters and some that arrive in East End waters through predictable annual migrations. Many of their fisheries quarries are migratory species that utilize vast areas of the East Coast as spawning and nursery areas, for feeding, and for migrating between and among these. As inshore or near shore fishers primarily, the baymen are affected by all of the activities on the land and within the watershed that surround their estuarine and marine fishing grounds on the East End.

The bay scallop on Long Island was a local fishery resource that was under considerable local control, although that control was mostly legal and regulatory. But there was a sense of "ownership" of the bay scallop resource by East Enders and the fishing community, and by other communities on Long Island where bay scallops occurred. Bay scallops provided a fairly reliable income each year for the baymen and were a source of local community identity. When the algal brown tide emerged and bloomed in the bays and estuaries during 1985, and a few subsequent years, it essentially put the local scallop fishery into a depleted-like or nearly collapsed status by killing off most of the local stock. That was an environmental and water quality issue that was out of the control of the fishing community. Prior to that event, the harvest of bay scallops from the East End's Peconic estuary system accounted for about 28% of the entire U.S. commercial harvest of bay scallops. It was a source of local pride and cultural identity.

On the East End

After the brown tide event, the entire East End community appeared to be different. Like the striped bass, the bay scallop seemed as a "numenon" of the East End estuaries and the East End fishing communities. It was an imponderable essence without which the whole system seemed empty and void. Without it, the fishermen, too, seemed empty and void. They seemed a bit wounded to me, wounded to the core of who they were, as inheritors of the trades of their fathers and grandfathers. They realized in fast order that their lives and livelihoods no longer were under their own independent control, as they has been for generations, since the marine and estuarine environment of the bays were changing. They, too, had to change, but not like their traditional ways of changing their fisheries and species with the seasons, but a change that was forced upon them due to human induced changes to the landscape, the watershed, and the marine environment. Their degraded capability to harvest from the East End waters was affected by all of the burgeoning activity in the watershed.

A degraded harvest by East End fishermen is not just an issue of their plight in these modern times, it is a symptom of much larger societal uses of and impact on the environment. These commercial fisheries, therefore, are a sort of "canary in the East End environmental mine." They are an indicator, a symptom, of the state of the entire ecological system, one that supported these fisheries for more than 200 years, but is doing otherwise now. We **all** should be concerned about this.

When the East Coast striped bass stock plummeted in the late 1970s and early 1980s, it was a regional coast-wide phenomenon that had local effects on the Long Island commercial and recreational fisheries, as well as similar effects to the fisheries on the whole mid-Atlantic seaboard. When that happened, a staple and reliable crop in the annual harvest of East End fishers was reduced drastically, and to the point that the entire East Coast fishery was closed to fishing and to harvest. That was another wound that affected the East End community and its identity. Again, it was a symptom of much larger societal uses of and impacts on the environment. It took Garrett Hardin's "mutual coercion, mutually agreed upon" in the form of a legally curtailed coast-wide harvest and subsequent heavy regulations to correct the fishery problem.

Compliance, Coercion, and Conservation

In 1968, Garrett Hardin published his classic account of a way we humans use natural resources and the environment. His account, entitled "Tragedy of the Commons," explained that people tend to use resources until the resources are economically depleted. This is done because people, in looking out for their own gain and survival, cannot self-regulate their behavior in a way that results in a sustainable resource. In order to use resources in a non-depleting manner, Hardin stated, people need a system of "mutual coercion, mutually agreed upon" (i.e., rules and regulations agreed to and enacted by society). While living by the rules, society somehow needs to turn the rules and regulations we use to protect the environment into values and ethics that informally govern society's interaction with resources and the environment, like those Maine lobstermen.

Hardin's "Tragedy of the Commons" today is not just what we take from the commons, but also what we put *into* the commons. Hardin explained it like this: "In a reverse way, the tragedy of the commons reappears in problems of pollution. Here it is not a question of taking something out of the commons, but of putting something in..." The lack of personal environmental ethics and the non-valuing of people are substantial causes of our tragedy of the commons, of our littering of the landscape, and our using and abusing of the environment. Laws, rules, and regulations cannot fix the absence of a community-focused environmental ethic for the commons. This must come through people valuing each other, and it must come through education and the mentoring of our children, so that they will grow up to value people and care for the environment, and not grow up to litter the landscape and pollute the resources.

Compliance with rules and regulations, alone, never is enough to ensure the quality and sustainability of both the environment and the ever expanding human enterprise that relies on the environment. Rules and regulations suggest, to many, that simply complying with the law, no more and no less, is all that is needed in order to protect the environment that sustains our very being. This tends to downplay personal obligation and responsibility, and places these on the back of government to enact and to enforce environmental protection, by rule of law and mutual coercion. Personal stewardship and an ethical relationship with the environment, nature, and Earth can be stifled by a belief that laws, lawsuits, and the courts are all that is needed.

In some ways, the compliance approach to environmental protection appears to be like a veneer. Compliance is like an outer coating, or veneer, that seems attractive and made to resemble something valued that is more substantial, and thus often is mistaken for more solid and quality protective beneath. An attractive outer surface (like veneer) suggests that the entire substance beneath is as the outer appearance. Veneer, however, can have little depth or strength. Like veneer, environmental compliance can lull the resource using public, and even the governmental environmental protection practitioner, into a false sense of believing that all is well beneath the surface. Sometimes the compliance approach seems like something that money and human resources were spent on in order to "buy" or purchase environmental protection, as with new technology, with environmental permits, with lengthy and expensive environmental impact statements, and even with compliance fines and penalties. It seems that we may be suffering from a "compliance syndrome" that keeps us from attaining a personal or community based stewardship approach to protection of the environment.

Going beyond compliance to a personal ethical relationship (i.e., stewardship approach) with the environment seems to be viewed as unnecessary, because there are many (some would say too many) coercive rules and regulations to do the protecting of the environment for us. I really believe that, in some ways, the compliance approach to environmental protection is but a nice looking veneer that is lulling us into a false sense of security about the future of our environment and natural resources. Most environmental laws seem to be a bit behind the times anyway. They often are reactionary and are created in response to a developing environmental problem or to a problem that already is existing, like the brown tide algal bloom or the waning striped bass fishery of the 1980s. A sad thing about this, also, is that Garrett Hardin still seems to be right.

If people despoil the landscape and the watershed as they use the environment, they not only devalue the environment, but they show their lack of valuing the people who would use the environment or the resource after them or along with them. Landscapes and environments despoiled by some people are not attractive for use by others. If the East End is not careful, the quality of its environment, that attracts people to it, may repulse them when it becomes despoiled. This thought deeply saddens me.

Without seeming to preach here, a Biblical corollary is explanatory. The New Testament describes the Greatest Commandment, as well as the second greatest, which are very simple in concept: love God, and love your neighbor. In practice, they may be very difficult, however. When it comes to stewardship of the environment, the ethic seems equally as simplistic, I believe: love the Creation (i.e., value nature, Earth, and the environment), and love the people (value people and the community who need and use the environment). Both are needed in order for wholeness to exist in both people and the environment. Loving, respecting, and valuing people must precede the loving and valuing of the Earth and its natural resources. When the people are whole and in community, the environment will follow suit.

These processes of healing and wholeness are immensely difficult, however, and require participation by all of society. All of the people, not just the fishing community or the local residents, with an interest in or a stake in the quality of the East End environment need to come together "in community" and work beyond the conservation and environmental rules and regulations in order to affect a whole and sustainable East End environment. Valuing each other and the commons must occur first and they must occur ***now***. All of the East End's stakeholders need to become an extended community group and exercise altruistic behavior in order to preserve, and indeed enhance, the East End's environmental commons.

The East End's stakeholders need a new or renewed environmental ethic for the commons, one that is collectively focused and mutually agreed upon. Professor Jonathan Haidt of the University of Virginia describes morality, including ethics and altruism, as the unifying principle among people because it binds and builds. He states that "a moral community has a set of shared norms about how members ought to behave, combined with means for imposing costs on violators and/or channeling benefits to cooperators." A renewed environmental ethic would help to bind and build a moral, or ethical and altruistic, community of East End stakeholders, while stewarding the environmental commons.

There always has been an environmental spirit among the East End people, but the everyday process of living and survival has dulled it a bit. And the influx of new citizenry has diluted it a bit. Amongst our living and surviving in our human society, we must also live and thrive amongst, and as part of, our natural community. Aldo Leopold said it aptly when he wrote of integrating our approach to living: "In addition to being conscious citizens of his political, social, and economic community, he should be a conscious citizen of

The Last Best Times?

Block Island Sound Vista. In this photo, my wife Mary and two friends, Alan and Celeste Steil, rest atop a Montauk hill, elevation 80 feet above sea level. We hiked Montauk in the fall of 1972 to overlook Shagwong Cove, Oyster Pond, and Block Island Sound. Along the way we passed Montauk's oldest tree, a nice understory of wild American holly, and some wetlands. This kind of environmental and outdoor activity was typical of the East End's local residents, as well as regular summer visitors, who appreciated the natural quality of landscape and seascape.

Admiring, appreciating, and respecting the environment are as much a part of protecting it as are rules, regulations, and laws. Environmental laws, however, are only the beginning of protecting the environment. They are the minimum of what needs to be done. People need to exercise a personal and ethical relationship with the environment in order to really protect it and steward it for the future.

his watershed, his migratory bird flyway, his biotic zone." I might paraphrase this a bit, in a corny way, to focus it on our East End living, particular in light of this discussion of the fishing community: "In addition to being conscious citizens of our human political, social, and economic communities, we should be conscious citizens of our East End watershed, our migratory fish pathways, our marine and estuarine biotic zones."

All of this is an immense challenge. Can it really happen? I am not so naïve as to think it will. But I have hope and I continue to strive toward these ends. The time is not for despair now, but for community-focused action and continued striving. We all are part of this current epic and all are a part of the eventual outcome.

Like a Wild Mustang

The land, water, and people of the East End have been an intertwined whole that now appears to be growing a bit weary, and becoming a bit disconnected. The Whole seems to be weeping collectively, silently. It has taken me more than 30 years of being away in order to really sense and hear this. It is related to the native East Enders who are fishers of the waters and tillers of the soil. They are the descendants of those Europeans who settled the East End and were befriended by the aboriginal inhabitants. Over the last several centuries, they have been in tune with the seasons, the tides, and they have understood the whims and moods of the ocean and its resources. The fishers have taken their troubles to the water, and it has calmed them. I have seen this first hand. I was one of those calmed by the East End's waters. It knew and understood me long before I really knew it. And now I hear it and sense its weeping. There has been a large population growth on the East End in recent years, and too many people on the East End now no longer understand. I think that too many of these people go to the land and to the water expecting something of its bounty, but giving little, and listening not at all. They do not let the lands and waters know them. It is a one sided relationship, the kind in which the land and sea always loose.

In his "Nature Notes" column of April 22, 1999, in the *East Hampton Star*, the venerable East End naturalist Larry Penny wrote of seeing and understanding clearly—for the first time,—the "ground

The Last Best Times?

Montauk Light in 1975. Whenever I am on the East End I always swing by to visit this old friend at the extreme eastern tip of Long Island and New York State. She was commissioned by George Washington in 1797 to last 200 years. Coastal lights such as this have watched over and protected us mariners for centuries. They stand as enduring traditional symbols of people helping people who work on the ocean environment. We have kept these old lights, restored them to their former glory, and we now watch over them and protect them from washing away into the sea. In just this same way we need to steward and nurture our traditional human treasures and historic symbols of our coastal communities — our traditional fisheries.

We need to keep them, protect them, restore them, and assure that they will not erode away and vanish into the sea. They are symbols of the wholeness of the environment and the wholeness of the human community. Valuing people and the environment involves stewarding both. When I think of Montauk Light's 200+ year existence at the edge of the sea, I am reminded as well of a 200+ year old East End human maritime community on the bluff overlooking the sea and teetering on the brink. All of the people with a stake in the environment of the East End need to come together as an extended community working as one to preserve and protect the environment we all hold in common.

war" on the East End. Larry was observing and surveying the East End from a helicopter. He wrote:

> [I] had heard about this ground war afoot, the one pitting naked land against naked money, but had been avoiding the precise points in the area where it was being waged. [I] always took the other roads, or took to looking the other way. Freud would call it repression. But from the air, the struggle in progress could not be hidden away. It was full-blown, it was awesome.... The earth below was under siege. It was being cleared, dug out, moved around, and built upon.... As we flew over, we could fairly hear the land groaning under the strain.

I sense that the East End organism still retains wildness and seems to be fighting back, yet, like a wild mustang trying to be tamed by its captor. There is a wild spirit left yet on the East End that is recognizable. There may be a human breaker aboard this old East End mustang, but she has not settled down, her spirit is not yet broken. She still fights to be wild, natural, free.

6

Eagles and Aborigines

I have known the East End since first going to live and work there in 1970. I have seen much of the East End's lands and waters and experienced many wonderful and strange things here. From nearly sinking on a fishing dragger, to lasting out a few nor'easters, to hearing a talking sea gull, to visiting friends in Amagansett's oldest (and haunted) house. But the most vexing and haunting memory I have is of the time, some years ago during a visit to the East End, when I met *Her*. I have written many pieces about the East End over time, on various subjects, but I have hesitated to write this one. It has been too disturbing, and I guess I figured that no one would really believe me. But the changing events and degradation of the land and marine environment in recent years, and its weeping I know that I sense, have suggested to me that I should relate this experience, for those who would read, and hear, and understand.

It was at Louse Point on Bonac Creek, fronting Gardiner's Bay, a place I know well and have visited often. I was walking along the sand spit, alone, at the harbor entrance, on the inside, around dusk. It was during early autumn; the tide was falling, hard. I was watching the sunset and skipping stones on the smooth and glassy water, when a strange feeling came over me. The kind of feeling you experience when you know, but don't immediately see, that someone is looking at you, watching you, maybe trying to silently get your attention. A chill went up my back, and I turned round quickly toward the east.

And I saw Her. She wasn't actually there. It was more like I experienced Her Presence. But She *was* visible, hauntingly so, with the light of the westerly setting sun enhancing her raiment of soft hues, very pleasing to the eye. I was aghast, and quivered in the evening chill; otherwise I was deathly motionless and silent. It was then that I realized the tide had ebbed, I think. At least the outward flow had ceased and the channel buoys were straight up and still. An eagle, yes an eagle, came into my view beyond Her. It was soaring, with motionless wings, in broad circles, probably above Napeague. It was the first eagle in flight that I had ever seen. And then the breeze subsided, as often happens with the change of tides. But this was very sudden, it seemed. And very different. It was a bit eerie, and a very awe inspiring. I looked round to see if anyone else was there. I was alone, in Her Presence.

She spoke softly and sweetly, in a way that commanded my attention to hear Her. I actually heard, or sensed, Her voice! Oh, my. Was I dreaming? No. But She sounded tired, I thought, or maybe elderly. Yes, the softness of Her voice was that of a gentle Elderly One, who speaks with slow purpose, from years of life's experience. It was as though She was talking through me, not directly to me. When Her eyes did focus on me, I turned away. I could not look directly into Her eyes, Her consciousness, Her soul. She spoke as a poet, sometimes not understandable, sometimes with discernible great wisdom. I do not recall all that She actually said, but rather retain a feeling of the essence of Her words, Her message, Herself.

She spoke of beginnings and endings, and many struggles. Of harmony and the stability of natural change. She reflected on the past, and spoke of the landscape and of the land meeting the sea. She mentioned something of the great whales. Of them She spoke so softly that I could not comprehend the thought. I wanted to speak up and question, but I dared not. The specific words I do recall were strange and hollow sounding. As She looked beyond me in an empty sort of stare, She said clearly, "I miss my eagles and my aborigines. We lived in harmony." It was then that I looked beyond Her for that soaring, circling eagle. It was not in my view. I wanted to tell Her that there *was* an eagle, still. It had arrived after Her, or perhaps came with Her. And that, yes, the aborigines were gone, but their descendents remained, along with descendents of those whom the aborigines had befriended.

As I looked away from the place of the soaring eagle, and back to Her, I felt Her once again looking into my eyes. I tried to speak, but could not. Her look was purposeful and powerful. I could not look away now, but tried. She spoke not of voice, but of expression and emotion. Her look was one of defined purpose, as though she was commanding me, willing me. It was also a look of tired desperation. "But what can *I* do?" I finally bleated out! "I am ... but one."

The breeze came up suddenly and I once again felt the chill. I looked quickly to the marker buoy in the inlet channel. It was leaning west; the tide was flooding, hard. I looked back quickly to eastward, into the empty evening sky. It was dimly lit by the reddish hue of the westerly setting sun. She was gone. I felt as though Her Presence had been with me for a season, yet it now seemed as though all had occurred within an eye's-wink of time.

I have returned to that place several times since, in hopes of seeing Her. I even went during early autumn, at dusk, on the ebbing tide. I never saw Her again. A few years later a brown tide appeared throughout the East End waters. The bay scallops vanished. Farmland had become fallow and disappeared. The whales are fewer. Descendents of the befriended have fallen on hard times. This may be their last real generation on the water. Where land meets sea, natural processes are interrupted, and great travails occur. Natural storms and fires have unnatural outcomes. The natural change is becoming unstable. Was She giving me a message? Sounding an alarm? Emoting a frustration … or gasping for breath. Why did She appear then, and to *me*? At times, I have doubted my own sanity in all of this, and I know some will think me mad. I have been haunted by Her absence ever since.

When I first penned some of these stories years ago, they ended with my haunting reflection of that fall on Louse Point. Since then I have pondered all of this over and over, for I have been deeply troubled with these matters seemingly having been left unfinished. I sensed that She wanted more of me in this, and to leave her message so incomplete went against my very nature in striving to be an instrument of environmental healing and stewardship. Her statement about eagles and aborigines living in harmony has held my attention all these years.

Why can't we twenty-first-century citizens of the East End, and indeed of Planet Earth, live in harmony with each other and our beloved landscape? Why can't we see beyond our immediate short-term existence? Her return … must be up to us, now. That's all I can figure. But to do that we have to get our own house in order first. Our relationships must be healed before we will be able to nurture Her and allow the wild mustang to remain free. But that's what makes

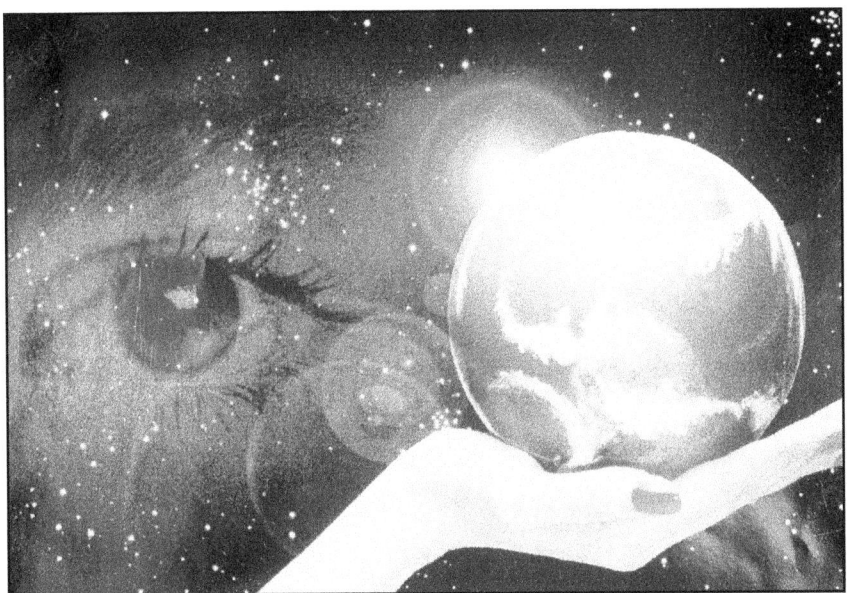

Listen and Hear.
Graphic courtesy of CLONTECH Laboratories, Inc., Palo Alto, CA.

this matter so difficult. We must hear and heal our own collective moaning before we will be able to really listen and truly hear the moaning of the land beneath us and the water around us. Too few are now in tune with what She has left us.

I am shivering as I write this. I still can see the buoys leaning hard and feel the chill of the wind, and I weep for my East End. I will return, sometime, and seek Her once again. Until then, I watch the eastern sky, hoping and praying that anyone who has an ear will listen to Her.

Bibliography & End Notes

The stories and accounts in this book are from my experiences living on Long Island's East End and working with those fishermen, baymen, baywomen, and other people mentioned throughout. My first person accounts of living on the East End are from the 1970s, with some updated information and discussion from subsequent visits in more recent years. All of those fishing accounts and stories are true. I have not annotated them, since they are my original experiences.

In this bibliography, I include reference sources on which I drew for information, especially related to my brief descriptions of the Long Island marine and estuarine environment, the watershed and landscape surrounding them, and sources related to current and future stewardship of those environs. This bibliography also includes many citations to papers and articles on fishes and the fisheries that resulted from the cooperation among many fishermen and scientists on the East End. All of the papers and articles that I authored and co-authored were placed into the Long Island Collection of the East Hampton Library. Copies also are contained in the public libraries of Amagansett and Montauk.

I have not provided here an in depth discussion of the many scientific studies done on the marine fisheries or on the history of scientific fisheries studies conducted on and around the East End. That was done in my 1985 "Special Report 65" published by the Marine Sciences Research Center of the State University of New York at Stony Brook. It is cited in the bibliography below. That survey report was updated and greatly expanded upon in 1997 by Michael J. Ahrens of the State

University of New York, Stony Brook, for the Peconic Estuary Program. Ahrens' annotated bibliography pulls together information on flora, fauna, natural habitats, ecology and environmental conditions of the Peconic Estuary and adjacent locations.

Acheson, James M. "Territories of the Lobstermen." *Natural History*. 81(4):60–69. 1972. Professor Acheson discusses the numerous traditional fishing norms by which the Maine lobstermen govern themselves, in addition to obeying the conservation laws.

Acheson, James M. "The Lobster Fiefs: Economic and Ecological Effects of Territoriality in the Maine Lobster Industry." *Human Ecology*. 3(3):183–207. 1975. Discusses the traditional norms, local voluntary conservation measures, the people of fishing community working together for the common good, and the economic and ecological effects of this behavior.

Ahrens, Michael. J. "An Annotated Bibliography of the Natural Resources of the Peconic Estuary and Adjacent Locations on Eastern Long Island." Marine Sciences Research Center, State University of New York, Stony Brook, NY. 1997. An annotated bibliography of 1317 literature references to the flora, fauna, natural habitats, ecology and environmental conditions of the Peconic Estuary and adjacent locations on the East End, prepared for the Peconic Estuary Program.

Austin, Herbert M. "Northern Range Extension of the Rhomboid Mojarra, *Diapterus rhombeus* Cuvier and Valenciennes (Gerridae)." *Chesapeake Science*. 14(3):22. 1973. This was the fish caught by bayman Tom Lester in his pound net.

Austin, Herbert M. and Clarence R. Hickey. "Migration and Mortality of Striped Bass Tagged in Eastern Long Island." pp. 11–16, *Fish Tag Seminar*. Published by the New York Ocean Science Laboratory (NYOSL). Symposium Sponsored by the American Littoral Society and NYOSL, 1974. This was a summary of our first three years of study of the migrations, growth, and abundance of striped bass in relation to the commercial fishery on the East End. I was the co-author on this paper with Herb Austin, but I analyzed and wrote much of it, with Herb's oversight and guidance. This is where I first wrote the analysis that became my *mea culpa* in trying to forecast the future of the striped bass fishery. I wrote: "Highly successful spawning and fingerling survival of striped bass in Chesapeake Bay has occurred at six-year intervals—1958, 1964, and 1970. If this pattern continues, the 1976 year class should be a successful and numerous brood. It appears, then, that the population of Chesapeake Bay striped bass, while naturally fluctuating, is numerous and healthy." The coastal population was indeed numerous, but the 1976 year class turned out not to be numerous and the Chesapeake Bay striped bass was at the beginning of a several year decline in spawning success with resulting and declining population abundance and fishery harvests. These declines became apparent within the next few years, and in 1985 the East Coast fishery was closed on a multi-state basis.

Austin, Herbert M. and Clarence R. Hickey, Jr. "Predicting Abundance of Striped Bass, *Morone saxatilis*, in New York Waters from Modal Lengths." *Fishery Bulletin*. 76 (2): 467–473. 1978. This paper describes the variations in the lengths of two-year-old striped bass caught in different years on eastern Long Island and relates that to the abundance of the fish there. It demonstrates statistically that when the spawning success was high and the surviving fingerlings were numerous, the striped bass were smaller at age 2, than were two-year-old striped bass from a less successful spawning when the fingerlings were less numerous. When there were more fish they were smaller, and when there were fewer fish they were larger. The striped bass that we studied were caught by bayman Jimmy Lester in his Fort Pond Bay, Montauk, pound nets in 1972, and by several haul seine crews on the ocean beaches of East Hampton Town in 1974. We were fortunate to have studied the striped bass when the coastal population and the fishery harvests were at their peaks in the early and mid-1970s.

Briggs, Philip T. and John R. Waldman. "Annotated List of Fishes Reported from the Marine Waters of New York." *Northeastern Naturalist*. 9(1): 47–80. 2002. Phil Briggs was a biologist (now retired) with the New York State Department of Environmental Conservation (DEC) and a very prolific author on marine fishery subjects. John Waldman is a scientist with the Hudson River Foundation in New York City and a research associate with the American Museum of Natural History in New York. This paper is the most recent and complete review and listing of the fish fauna known to occur in the marine waters of New York State. 338 species of fishes are documented. More than 200 fish species have been recorded and reported from the waters of the East End, which includes portions of Long Island Sound, Block Island Sound, and the Atlantic Ocean, as well as the Peconic and Gardiner's Bay system. Several of the papers that were written by the baymen and me are included in the listing. I was privileged to offer review and comment to Briggs and Waldman on a latter version of their manuscript prior to publication.

Cole, John. *Striper: A Story of Fish and Man*. Atlantic-Little, Brown Books. New York. 1978. In this classic book, the author recalls his days commercial fishing for striped bass on the East End in the 1950s. He discusses striped bass natural history and offers a warning about the effects of environmental degradation on the striped bass.

Despres, Linda. "NOAA Ship *Albatross IV.*" Woods Hole Historical Museum, Massachusetts. Undated. This report describes the 45-year operational history of this research vessel, on which I sailed in 1974. *Albatross IV* was commissioned in 1963 and decommissioned in 2008. The report also contains a remembrance, written by scientist Henry Jensen, of biologist Robert Hersey who was the person remembered in the burial at sea I witnessed. That ceremony occurred on March 29, 1974, 75 miles south of Martha's Vineyard.

East Hampton Star. Obituaries and articles on the passing of local fishing family persons including: Kathryn M. Lester (January 29, 1981); William J. Lester, "Cap'n Bill" (January 31, 1991); Norman C. Edwards (May 22, 1997); Thomas E. Lester (October 15, 1992); Cathy Lester (November 24, 2005); William E. Havens (June 15, 2006); Vernon Jarvis Wood (January 18, 2007); Calvin Gray Lester (August 9, 2007); Frank Mundus (September 18, 2008); Lottie A. Lester, Cap'n Bill's wife (March 17, 2011); Milton L. Miller (December 20, 2012); Peter Matthiessen (April 10, 2014); Benjamin J. Havens (September 4, 2014); Milton M. George (September 18, 2014).

Epstein, John and Elizabeth Barlow. *East Hampton: A History and Guide.* Medway Press, Inc., East Hampton. 1975. A local history book on the Town of East Hampton "for the armchair visitor and resident … also meant to be a sightseer's guide." It discusses the history and the places of Montauk and Fort Pond Bay.

Haidt, Jonathan. "The New Synthesis in Moral Psychology." *Science.* 316 (5827): 998–1002. 2007.

Hardin, Garrett. "Tragedy of the Commons." *Science.* 162:1243–1248. 1968. This is Hardin's seminal and classic paper of people using the environmental commons. As people use the resource commons for their own gain and survival, the commons become depleted and ruined. Because populations of people cannot control their own resource use behavior, they must institute "mutual coercion, mutually agreed upon by the majority of the people affected." This coercion is in the form of public laws for the protection of the environment and use of natural resources.

Hickey, Clarence R., Jr. "Investigation and Analysis of a Mass Mortality of Commercial Lobsters (*Homarus americanus*) in Seabrook Harbor, New Hampshire, during October of 1977." NUREG-0468. Office of Nuclear Reactor Regulation, U.S. Nuclear Regulatory Commission, Washington, DC. 93 pp. 1978.

Hickey, Clarence R., Jr. "Water Mass Movement and the Migration of Striped Bass Around Eastern Long Island, New York." *New York Fish and Game Journal.* 28 (1): 108–114. 1981.

Bibliography & End Notes

Hickey, Clarence R., Jr. "Comparative Hematology of Wild and Captive Cunner." *Transactions of the American Fisheries Society*. 111 (2): 242–249. 1982. This paper resulted from my 1970 master's thesis at Long Island University. It describes how I was able to achieve a 95% survival rate among my experimental fishes and then return them alive to the marine environment.

Hickey, Clarence R., Jr. "Power Plant Siting and Design: A Case Study of Intake and Discharge Effects at Point Beach Nuclear Plant on Lake Michigan Biota and Fisheries." NUREG-0816. Office of Nuclear Reactor Regulation, U.S. Nuclear Regulatory Commission, Washington, DC. 53 pp. 1982. This report describes an example in which the conduct of certain fish netting studies to understand the environmental effects of a power plant on fishes (of Lake Michigan in this case) caught more fishes than were estimated to have been affected by operations of the power plant.

Hickey, Clarence R. "Survey of the Technical Literature on the Marine Finfishery Resources of the Peconic/Gardiner's Bay System, New York, 1900–1984, with Recommendations for Resource Conservation and Study." Special Report 65. Marine Sciences Research Center, State University of New York at Stony Brook. 106 pp. 1985. I wrote this technical report after I read an environmental report by Long Island Lighting Company (LILCO) on its Jamesport Nuclear Power Plant site on Long Island Sound. LILCO stated that there was not much information known about the environment at and near Jamesport, located in Riverhead Town on the North Fork. My 1985 report lists and describes 183 historical studies of the finfishes of the eastern Long Island marine environs.

Hickey, Clarence R. "Ocean Sciences Reminiscences." *East Hampton Star*, New York. Pages II-1 and II-18. October 31, 1985. This article is a nostalgic look back at the New York Ocean Science Laboratory (NYOSL) on Montauk, a former coastal marine research laboratory, its programs, and people. I worked at NYOSL from 1970 to 1975.

Hickey, Clarence R. "The Nearest Lighthouse." *Fisheries*, A Bulletin of the American Fisheries Society. 13(4): 22–24. 1988. This is a photo essay of lighthouses I have encountered while traveling along the east and west coasts and the Great Lakes. My photo of Montauk Light was on the cover of this issue of the Bulletin.

Hickey, Clarence R. "Fish on the Muffler." In: *Sea Fare—The Official American Fisheries Society Cookbook*. Volume I, Chapter 4, page 57. 1991. This is an article, a true tale, about cooking fresh fish at sea on a work boat's hot muffler. Bayman Jimmy Lester told me about this cooking procedure, so I tried it on the dragger *Lady Barbara* and then wrote about how to do it for the AFS, one of the professional scientific societies to which I belong.

Hickey, Clarence R. "First, Do No Harm." *NAAS News*, Newsletter of the National Association of Academies of Science, published quarterly. 3(4): 3-4. Fall 2000. This is an article on the environmental responsibility of scientists, with an environmental charge and challenge to students. It was adapted from a lecture I give to the National Association of Academies of Science and the American Junior Academy of Sciences, that was held in conjunction with the 2000 Annual Meeting of the American Association for the Advancement of Science in Washington, DC. The article draws upon my experiences in trying to be more humane to captured fishes and to take only those fishes needed for study, returning the rest to the marine environment.

Hickey, Clarence R. "First, Do No Harm." *BRIEFS*, Newsletter of the American Institute of Fishery Research Biologists (AIFRB). 29(6): 4-5. 2000. This was a reprinted version of the above article in the *NAAS News*, which I shared with the AIFRB, of which I am a member. The AIFRB is a professional association of fishery researchers that is concerned about professionalism and ethics.

Hickey, Clarence R., Jr. and Richard A. Amish. "Stunted Growth of a Jawless Striped Bass, *Morone saxatilis*. *Transactions of the American Fisheries Society*. 104 (2): 410-412. 1975.

Hickey, Clarence R., Jr. and James W. Lester. "Notes on Lumpfish from Montauk, New York." *New York Fish and Game Journal*. 22 (2): 164-166. 1975.

Hickey, Clarence R., Jr. and James W. Lester. "Marine Fishes of Southern Origins in New York Waters and Their Contribution to the Fishery." *New York Fish and Game Journal*. 27 (1): 99-102. 1980.

Hickey, Clarence R., Jr. and James W. Lester. "The Fishes of Fort Pond Bay on Long Island, New York" *New York Fish and Game Journal*. 30 (1): 100-112. 1983. I began writing this compilation of the fishes in 1975 while I still was on the East End, but I did not complete it until several years later. In this paper, bayman Jimmy Lester and I annotate the presence and seasonal abundance of 102 fish species caught in Fort Pond Bay during 1970-1978.

Hickey, Clarence R., Jr. and James W. Lester. "Additional Records of Fishes from Fort Pond Bay on Long Island, New York." *American Currents*. 24 (2): 6-10. 1998. This is a follow up to the 1983 paper above. It adds six more species to the list of fish fauna in Fort Pond Bay, for a total of 108, and covers the time period of 1970-1981.

Hickey, Clarence R., Jr. and Thomas E. Lester. "First Record of the Gizzard Shad from Long Island, New York." *New York Fish and Game Journal*. 23 (2): 188-189. 1976.

Bibliography & End Notes

Hickey, Clarence R., Jr. and Bradley Loewen. "New Record for the Greater Amberjack from New York Waters." *New York Fish and Game Journal.* 23 (2): 184–185. 1976.

Hickey, Clarence R., Jr., Allan D. Sosnow and James W. Lester. "Pound Net Catches of Warm-Water Fishes at Montauk, New York." *New York Fish and Game Journal.* 22 (1): 38–50. 1975

Hickey, Clarence R. and Byron H. Young. "Incidence of Morphological Abnormalities in Striped Bass from the Hudson River and Coastal Long Island, New York." *New York Fish and Game Journal.* 31(1): 104–108. 1984. This report resulted from the observations made by the authors and their colleagues during biological and population studies of striped bass caught by commercial haul seine and by beach seine in the mid-to late 1970s. This is an example of the New York State DEC and the Montauk Lab biologists examining catches of striped bass for the health conditions of the fish and then sharing new or important information openly and publicly.

Hickey, Clarence R., Jr., Byron H. Young and James W. Lester. "Tarpon from Montauk, New York." *New York Fish and Game Journal.* 23 (2): 186–187. 1976. This short paper documents the capture by commercial fishermen of two tarpon from the marine waters of Montauk in 1974. One was caught by bayman Jimmy Lester in his pound net in Fort Pond Bay during July. The second was caught by bayman Dominic Grace's haul seine crew on the ocean beach at Montauk during August. Byron Young was with the haul seiners that day and they were able to release the tarpon alive after measuring and weighing it.

Hickey, Mary T. "Age, Growth, Reproduction and Distribution of the Bay Scallop, *Aequipecten irradians* (Lamarck), in Three Embayments in Eastern Long Island, New York, as Related to the Fishery." Master's Thesis, C.W. Post College, Long Island University. 1977. This field research study was conducted during 1974 and coincided with the peak year in bay scallop commercial landing in New York State. In 1985 the brown tide algae bloom appeared in East End waters and killed so many scallops that the population essentially was depleted and of no commercial value.

Holden, Albert R. *A Pictorial History of Montauk.* Holden Publications, Montauk. 1983. A history of Montauk in pictures, maps, and text from the mid-1600s to the 1980s.

Jensen, Albert C. "New York's Marine Fisheries: Changing Needs in a changing Environment." *New York Fish and Game Journal.* 24(2): 99–128. 1977.

Jentoft, Svein. "Healthy Fishing Communities: An Important Component of Healthy Fish Stocks." *Fisheries.* 24(5):28–29. 1999. The author argues for inclusion of social concerns and a focus on community as part of fisheries regulation and management. He states that fisheries management is about governance of human behavior, not fish behavior.

Leopold, Aldo. *A Sand County Almanac with Essays on Conservation from Round River.* Ballantine Books and the Oxford University Press. 1970. This is an enlarged edition of Leopold's original 1949 book *A Sand County Almanac and Sketches Here and There.* It combines all of the *Almanac* with eight essays from Leopold's 1953 book *Round River.*

Matthiessen, Peter. *Men's Lives: The Surfman and Baymen of the South Fork.* Random House, New York. 1986. The author of this classic and monumental book worked as a commercial fisherman on the East End in the mid-1950s. It is a documentary, written in the early 1980s, about the East End fishermen, their history and culture, and their struggles fishing amid the high cost of living in the Hamptons, increasing environmental degradation, and restrictive environmental laws. I was privileged to write a book review on *Men's Lives* for the American Fisheries Society which published it in the Bulletin *Fisheries* 12(3): 61, 1987.

"Nixon, Charles H. "Sailing Order NOAA Ship Albatross IV, Cruise 74-4, Part II." U.S. Department of commerce, Northeast Marine Support Facility. March 22, 1974. This is the operational cruise plan and sailing order for the March 26–April 11, 1974 research cruise on which I participated.

Pajak, Paul. "Sustainability, Ecosystem Management, and Indicators: Thinking globally and Acting Locally in the 21st Century." Fisheries. 25(12):16–30. 2000. The author argues for a blending of scientific, technical, and social processes to affect positively the sustainability of environmental resources. He states "the overwhelming majority of daily decisions cumulatively affecting global and local sustainability tend to be made by individual people … a concerned public will probably need a better way to visualize the 'big picture,' that is, the consequences of their behavior on the ecological and social sustainability of their local communities, watersheds, region, and so on."

Peconic Baykeeper. "Baywatch: Long Island's Bay Health Report 2006." This is the first report on the health of Long Island's Peconic and South Shore Bays since the founding of the Baykeeper program in 1997. This report rates the quality of the environmental conditions and natural resources, including local fisheries, of the bays "by measuring the findings against their counterparts in the 1970s, when recorded commercial and recreational landings of selected finfish and shellfish were at their peak and the bays were by all other verifiable standards healthy and productive."

Bibliography & End Notes

Peconic Estuary Program. "Peconic Estuary Comprehensive Conservation and Management Plan." 866 pp. Sponsored by the United States Environmental Protection Agency under Sec. 320 of the Clean Water Act. Suffolk County Department of Health Services, Program Office. 2001.

Penny, Larry. "Here Come the Spring Beasties." *East Hampton Star*. Page D11. March 8, 2007. In this issue of his weekly Nature Notes column, the naturalist author discusses the coming of spring with several of the East End's coastal ponds opening to the sea thus allowing the influx of migrating fishes. Fort Pond and its historical seasonal inlet to Fort Pond Bay, prior to the coming of the railroad in the late 1800s, are discussed.

Sterling, Dorothy. *The Outer Lands: A Natural History Guide to Cape Cod, Martha's Vineyard, Nantucket, Block Island, and Long Island*. The Natural History Press, Garden City, New York. 1967.

Warner, William. *Beautiful Swimmers: Watermen, Crabs and the Chesapeake Bay*. Penguin Books, New York. 1976.

Weiner, Sandra. *I Want to be a Fisherman*. Macmillan Publishing Co., Inc., New York. 1977. A true story using text and photos about an 11-year-old girl who fishes with her bayman father at his fish traps (pound nets) in the waters of the South Fork of the East End in the 1970s.

Young, Byron H. "Species Composition of Surf Waters at Montauk 1973-1975." Unpublished data from the New York State DEC, Stony Brook, New York. 1976. Young and associates observed the presence of 76 species of fishes in the haul seine catches of commercial fishermen along the Atlantic Ocean beaches of Montauk.

Young, Byron H. "Cubera Snapper from New York Waters." *New York Fish and Game Journal*. 25(1):84. 1978. This fish was caught by bayman Jimmy Lester in his pound nets in Fort Pond Bay, Montauk.

Young, Byron H, Frederick M. Mushacke, and Michael Litwa. "A New Isopod parasite of Striped Bass." *New York Fish and Game Journal*. 31(1): 116-118. 1984. One of the striped bass found with this parasite was captured by haul seine in the Atlantic Ocean near Amagansett. This is an example of the New York State DEC biologists examining catches of striped bass for the health conditions of the fish and then sharing new or important information openly and publicly.

Young, Byron H., Bruce Ringers, Thomas W. Woithe, and Charles T. Hamilton. "Striped Bass and the Sport Fishery During Daylight Hours From 1973 to 1975 at Montauk, New York." *New York Fish and Game Journal*. 33(2): 124-147. 1986. This paper resulted from the New York State DEC's robust studies of striped-bass fishery harvests during the 1970s, in this case the sport fishery in the Montauk area. The paper states that the study "was begun just as the population [of striped bass] reached a peak [in 1973] and was beginning to decline." It also asserted that "If the catch statistics for the sport fishery had included these other areas [of Long Island's marine waters beyond Montauk], it is estimated that the landings would have been equal to or greater than those of the commercial fishermen." With "the significant role that the sport fishery plays in the harvest of striped bass … the sport fishery must assume responsibility to a significant degree for management measures applied to the total fishery for striped bass." Young and associates observed that 26 species of fishes were caught by boat anglers and surf anglers in the waters surrounding Montauk. This paper appeared in the last issue of the *Journal*.

Bibliography & End Notes

About the Author

Clarence Hickey holds a Master of Science degree in marine biology from Long Island University. His master's thesis research studied the blood physiology of fish from Long Island's estuarine waters. From 1970 to 1975 Clarence worked as a marine biologist on the staff of the New York Ocean Science Laboratory on Montauk. While at the Laboratory, Clarence joined with several local Baymen to study the marine fishes of the East End. They authored several papers on the natural history of the fishes in the *Fish and Game Journal*.

In 1983, Clarence and Bayman Jimmy Lester published a paper that annotated the presence and seasonal abundance of 102 fish species caught in Jimmy's trap nets in Fort Pond Bay between 1970 and 1978. In 1998, they updated that list of fishes to 108 species through 1981. During his time on the East End, Clarence was a member of the East Hampton Town Baymen's Association and a share holder in the East Hampton Town Seafood Producers Cooperative.

Clarence has more than 150 publications in scientific and conservation journals and elsewhere. He was a contributor to the *East Hampton Star* for many years in the 1980s and 1990s.

www.ingramcontent.com/pod-product-compliance
Lightning Source LLC
Chambersburg PA
CBHW050635160426
43194CB00010B/1677